A
MOURNING
MIRACLE

...the Dawning of my Dance

Reconstruction is more than coping; it is making meaning of the scattered pieces of life.
— Gulledge on Neimeyer

Elegantly weaving scholarly study with her own narrative, Dr. Dee encourages us not just to survive the grief experience, but to actually thrive as a result of doing the "hard work" of grief. Loss and grief affect every aspect of life – the way we think, the way we feel, and our physical, spiritual, and relational well-being. Learning to acknowledge and express the change in our lives, and to release the painful experience, is instrumental in re-creating life after loss.

A MOURNING MIRACLE

the Dawning of my Dance

Delores Dalrymple Gulledge

2013

 A MOURNING MIRACLE ~
the Dawning of my Dance

Advance Reader Comments:

"Dee taught me grief is hard work. I didn't understand why I was tired all the time. Now I relate to others the things she taught me. No one understands unless they have been there."
-*Caryl Gayle,* Bereaved Mother, Broker-in-Charge, Russell & Jeffcoat Real Estate Incorporated, Irmo, SC

"While others sidestep the issues of unanswered sorrow and grief, Dee intentionally walks into the middle of it. She takes you by the hand and exposes a larger and deeper world in which we all must travel sooner or later. She allows you to stand with her in that 'in-between' place where you look toward heaven with hands outstretched while life is not what you want it to be. The struggle, pain, honesty and eventual road to survival are documented with the hope that others might find their way too."
-*Dr. Ed Carney,* Senior Pastor, Riverland Hills Baptist Church, Irmo, S.C.

"I am moved beyond words that are adequate...you live the work we do. This is a story of healing when we as professionals struggle to give definition to the process. This book is raw and intimate, yet filled with hope, steadfastness, reverence, and endurance. It is absolutely inspirational. What a gift Melanie's life and death have given to all of us who are moved to make something meaningful of our own silent tragedies."
-*Dr. Peggy P. Whiting*, Professor and Coordinator of Counselor Education, North Carolina Central University

"Like any mother, I already adore my daughter. But reading of Dee's love for Melanie, and her boundless grief over the loss of her daughter, gave me a fresh infusion of tenderness and gratitude towards my Hannah. It also spurred in me an intense, gripping sense of the sacredness of every moment with her — that not a day should pass without a recognition of how fleeting all of life truly is, and how tightly, indeed intentionally, we are to seize the days with our precious ones."
-*Amanda Phifer*, Columbia, S.C

"I was honored to be asked to read Dr. Gulledge's book after observing her courage and commitment to complete her "grief song" journey and share it with others in need. The questions asked and releases she acknowledged proved very cathartic for me in examining my own response to the death of my beloved mother. Her insights about the grief journey also helped me to increase my understanding and sensitivity toward a close friend who lost her son in years past and most recently her husband."
-*Jan Mathias*, Retired Teacher

Acknowledgements

I wish to express appreciation for my family, a unique and special gift from God. And others who helped nurture a vision into reality.

For Melanie, my daughter who taught me to treasure every moment, value every relationship, dance to the music in my soul, and never give up.

For Christopher, my son who taught me that love and action on behalf of one can benefit many – if it's important to me then go after it.

For Alyssa, my daughter-in-law who demonstrates creative genius by transforming raw sheared wool into garments of beauty.

Most of all - For Van, my loving husband who models no task is too small to do well. He is like a tree planted by rivers of living water, always bearing fruit. His committed love, support and encouragement know no end. I look forward to continuing the years of our lives, sealed in service together.

For my Mother, the family matriarch, who modeled the struggle and search for her "own self" after my Daddy's death. Having recently celebrated her 90th birthday she continues to model living with a purpose, a caring heart and warm smile.

Acknowledgements

For my sisters and friends – Belinda Woods, artist of cover painting; Jenny Dalrymple, Jan Baker, book title; Gail Miller, Jan Mathias, Diane Croft, assistants with workshops, seminars, retreats.

For my brothers-in-law, nieces and nephews who have offered supportive encouragement through the years. For Al Miller's music and Gail Miller's sign language at special events.

For Marjory Ward, my patient mentor, prayer partner and friend for a lifetime.

For all my friends who have loved, encouraged, supported and prayed for me throughout this transformational process of discovery.

For my editor, graphic designer, layout designer and advance readers: I express appreciation for your investment in this multifaceted project.

"You can do it Mama. You can do it! Come on Mama, You can do it," clapped Melanie from her wheelchair.

"Blessed are they that mourn for they shall be comforted."   *Matthew 5:4 KJV*

Dedicated to Melanie,
a young woman of beauty and grace
always with a smiling face.
A daughter joyful for life,
proud of her brother,
giver of self,
dedicated to dance,
committed to Christ,
a pearl of great price.

A MOURNING MIRACLE
the Dawning of my Dance

CONTENTS

Preface   xiii

The Action of Survival   15

The Intentional Action of Reconstructing Life   25

The Intentional Action of Relearning My World   37

The Intentional Action of Reestablishing Relationships   47

The Intentional Action of Rebirthing a Place for Melanie   73

The Intentional Action of Reinventing Myself   89

Grief Survival Guide: When You Lose Someone You Love   101

The Intentional Action of Re-Creating the Story through "Griefsong"   125

The Intentional Action of Releasing the Story through "Griefsong"   135

The Intentional Action of Expressing Deep Personal Feelings through "Griefsong"   143

The Intentional Action of Conclusion   153

Epilogue – Serendipity of Reverberations   163·

Afterword
Dr. Dee's Dream   169

CONTENTS

Bibliography   173

Endnotes   177

About the Author   183

Preface

Dance your way through darkness of grief into the mourning/morning light.

Grasp the glimpses of light and flashes of joy as you work to turn your mourning into dancing.

Melanie asked, "Mama, how will people ever know what this is like?" I replied, "We will teach them, Sweetheart. Perhaps one by one, but we will teach them."

I wanted to write a descriptive narrative, an honest account, of my personal journey as a means of offering inspiration and hope to others. I wanted grieving people to know there can be life after the death or loss of someone or something invaluable. I wanted this effort to encourage others to open up to creativity and appreciate the glimpses of light and search for the flashes of joy along the mourning way. I wanted to demonstrate and support creative and expressive arts as avenues for grief expression. I wanted to educate about the grief experience and process and to help those who are grieving explore ways to reach reconciliation.

Reconstruction of life after loss is more than coping; it is gathering the shattered and scattered pieces of life to make meaning from the loss experience. My narrative supports the concept of grieving as a meaning-making process.

Encouragement for intentional action for positive growth does not minimize the depth of grief soul pain. Just as the dawn from on high breaks to give light to those who sit in darkness, it is my hope that the dawn of healing will emerge from your grief wilderness.

Delores Dalrymple Gulledge, Ph.D.
Arts as Medicine, llc

THE ACTION OF SURVIVAL

The survival period is the time when you're gasping and grasping, groping to order thoughts enough to accomplish the tasks at hand.

We stayed with Melanie in her room in the hospital – "The Room of Light" – for six hours after her final breath. It was a time of transformation we were allowed to witness. I gave her over into the arms of Jesus. Her Daddy verbalized his love and apologized for his shortcomings—where he had failed her. My son, Christopher, wept beside her bed.

I wondered, what was wrong with me? Why didn't I weep and wail and grieve? Where were my tears?

Those who have studied this grief process tell us that for us to be able to resolve our grief; we need to recognize the loss. In our case I didn't want to admit our daughter no longer lived on this earth. In fact, when my husband walked around the corner with the doctor and said, "Dee, she is gone. Melanie is gone. They did all they could, but she is gone." I responded, "No! No! No! It cannot be!

Let's go see what we can do. God can do it...and He promised."

I refused to leave her in the hospital alone; she had not been alone up to that point, and I certainly did not intend to leave her alone now. We stayed with her for six hours—it was precious time—as we waited for the funeral home personnel to arrive. I sent someone for a camera to capture that heart-rending moment on film.

Van and I knew we would not be returning to the hospital with Melanie. It was important to us to express our gratitude for the care she had received there. As we were leaving, we asked if we could leave a note on the board in the nurses' station. I wrote in detail thanking the doctors, nurses, support personnel and cleaning ladies for their care and concern for our precious daughter and for us. It was a strange feeling, a sort of finality, knowing this thank you would be our last connection with the caregivers on Melanie's behalf. We were later told the note remained intact for two months. They somehow felt it was almost sacred, and no one wanted to erase it. Then finally one day it too was gone.

Those next days could have been a blur; however I remember them in great detail. My husband directed the friends who rushed into our home to break down the hospital bed to get it moved out of the family room. They moved the emergency oxygen tank out also, in an attempt to return the room to normal. But, what is normal?

I called my friend Carolyn to say, "She's gone! Melanie is gone home to be with Jesus." She offered to skip school, but I insisted that she go ahead with her daily teaching responsibilities, suggesting she come by in the afternoon on her way home instead. "It will be a busy day," I told her.

We arrived home supposedly to sleep a few hours, but sleep would not be so kind to me – my mind was full. There were so many things to do.... take clothes to the funeral home. There was not really a contest as to how to dress her. There it was – her dress, her special dress. The one she selected for her Modeling Extravaganza. She also wore it at Easter with the stylish straw hat, so proud and beautiful. And the prom, of course, the prom. That special evening when the theme was "A Night To Remember." She was so beautiful with her handsome date. He had for her not only a corsage of peach colored roses, but also an extra special gift

17

like none other. A piece of jewelry designed for her with qualities and detail as unique as the one it was designed for. There seemed to be a moment in time when the clock stopped as her date dropped on one knee before her presenting her with the special gift. Her delight, her joy, her satisfaction were matched only by those observing as the pearl ring was removed from its velvet lined box and placed on her finger – her index finger. There it was – a pearl of great price, for a young woman like none other on earth. Her dancing eyes, admiring the gift, darted from the ring to the face of her date as she exclaimed, "Thank you, Daddy. Thank you so much. Now, let's go to the prom."

Selecting the casket: We were invited into a great room filled with large box-shaped beds called caskets. There were choices, so many choices—different designs, materials, and colors. We must select something worthy of her.

It seems such a bizarre concept for the grief stricken to struggle for survival even as they visit a funeral home to make choices about arrangements to accommodate the deceased over the next few days. And to select a container that will hold the remains of the one held so dear.

Laura, Melanie's private duty nurse, bathed her as usual on that Wednesday morning. This would be their last bath together. It took place in the sterility of the funeral home. Audrey, Melanie's hairdresser, shampooed, dried and arranged her hair, as was her custom on her day off.

After these things had been done and the embalming process completed, she was dressed in her beautiful, special dress and her shoes.

I applied her make-up, talking to her all the while. My sister, Gail, polished her fingernails. My sister, Belinda, came for the final moments as we were putting on her pearl necklace and earrings and placing that very special ring on her finger.

It felt like playing dress-up with a life-sized porcelain doll. My sister, Jenny, and my Mother did not come to the funeral home at this time to share this part of the ritual. They joined us later.

I photographed our beautiful bride-like daughter.

We were not rushed. When we felt finished, the funeral home director requested a few minutes to arrange her in her final bed, the bronze casket fit for a princess.

After a short time, the woman who had helped settle her into the casket opened the doors breathlessly, approaching us with eyes wide and hands outstretched before her, saying, "I've just had the most profound experience of my life. I feel as if I have just touched something pure, holy, and virginal." To which I responded, "You have, my dear, you have." We all sensed the sacred presence of holiness.

There were more details that required attention, including writing the newspaper announcement of her death. I felt I must do it myself. I felt urgency and responsibility to be sure everything that was done was honoring to the person of Melanie.

People, so many people, came to express their regret. They came to console and to comfort. But I had no tears. I had so many things to think about. I wanted everything to be perfect concerning the service. I became the consoler and the comforter. Then I excused myself to be alone. One friend asked if I wanted her to change the sheets on Melanie's bed. She had done it often before, so I said yes. I knew another friend would handle the kitchen.

It was only the beginning of a parade that wanted to offer support and needed to express their personal sense of loss from Melanie's death. People came from church, community, school, and the hospital. There were adults, students, and children (who did not understand her death). Relatives, friends, acquaintances, professionals, laborers and the retired were among the mass of people. They all came, to hug, to weep, and to speak or not. As is sometimes the case, my senses were hyper-mobilized. I remember my dress, my fragrance and the thought that Melanie would be pleased by the care of my personal appearance for her friends and mine. Our home was open, and our shattered hearts receptive. Only God could have created that atmosphere. There were so many decisions; I even considered having the casket in our home, as was the custom when I was a child. Those were only the preliminary stages. Life without Melanie had not yet registered on the seismograph of life.

Melanie's funeral service provided a vehicle for the expression of feelings without words in interpretive dance. Her brother sang. Her Daddy read a poem written by one of Melanie's friends. I read the Old Testament Psalm 24, the basis for the dance.

At the suggestion of a friend, a display honoring some special events and accomplishments in Melanie's life was arranged. We selected representative items from Melanie's room, and our creative friends placed them appropriately.

Hundreds, and hundreds, and hundreds visited to offer their hugs and sympathy. Some folks stood in line four or five hours. Many left because they were unable to wait. For five hours, people paraded by us. There were Melanie's friends, Christopher's friends and our friends. Many lived near; some traveled several hours to reach us.

Many people we didn't even know shared cards of comfort and encouragement in support of our loss. Boxes and boxes are packed away.

Riverland Hills Baptist Church had never had so many people fill its pews for a funeral service before this time.

The graveside service afforded the opportunity for those in our home community, two hours away from Columbia, to also share this time with us.

We were active participants in church. Faith community members responded to Melanie's death by gathering around us week after week speaking words of encouragement. They mourned her death in a variety of ways, including flowers, meals, and contributions to specific faith-based funds as well as scholarships. They also were generous with tears, hugs and sharing by talking about Melanie, showing interest in where we, the parents, were speaking, and what we were doing.

Even survival itself seemed to be a constant battle. From time to time it all just continued to seem too much – too overwhelming – and I wondered if I would be sad forever. At first I didn't want to acknowledge the sadness. I put on a bright smile to cover the pain and went out to face the world as I knew it. Accounts of the grief of others indicate that some cry every day for weeks on end. My pain was so deep there were no tears to express it.

There were so many questions without answers. The search seemed continuous in the Scriptures, in medical research, in life. Sitting, walking, standing, leaping, running…there seemed to be no escape. How does one manage the internal turmoil, the external emptiness, life that seemingly has lost its meaning?

Researchers suggest that some mothers cope by using humor while others cope by making "downward comparisons"[1] suggesting ways that could have made the situation worse. Others try to understand or make meaning out of the death. I took intentional actions to make something good come out of a devastating situation.

THE INTENTIONAL ACTION
OF
RECONSTRUCTING LIFE

Life as I knew it began to deconstruct with Melanie's diagnosis.

My intentional actions of reconstructing, relearning, rebirthing and reinventing are separate entities that are also rewoven together into a bigger whole. The telling of the story may help one reconstruct her world. When a life is interrupted by a loss, it disrupts the whole of that life. The fragmented life must be reconstructed to maintain a link from the past to the future.

Reconstruction is more than coping; it is making meaning of the scattered pieces of life.

People are excellent at responding immediately after death; however I believe they are less skilled at follow-up after the funeral. I felt like I was on an island with a fragmented life, trying to fit the pieces back together alone. Parents feel disassociated in the internal and external world. For the social reality of the child's death, parents need validation of their loss. They need to know others care about and share the loss. Parents need validation that they really hurt. It is difficult to be in a group where people seem to purposefully avoid saying the name or mentioning the life of the deceased. It seems as if others are ignoring the hurt of the loss. Sometimes a parent may feel a sense of isolation even in a crowded room. The child is dead, never to return again, but the bond of love still connects parent to child. Because the community as a whole does not understand the experience of loss, parents receive little help from others as they try to make sense of their loss.

The question returns again and again: How do I go on when beliefs about the world seem to be in so many pieces and none of the pieces seem to make sense? It seems as if I'm living in a parallel universe. One seems to call me to old habits, beliefs and relationships, while the forming universe calls me into the unknown darkness of shadows, questions and isolation where I seem to wander in lostness, groping for what must only be vestiges of the past. It causes me to wonder where I really belong. I can no longer live in my past world since it has changed forever. I do not know how to make my way in the world that is before me.

Who will help me? Who will show me the way? And then I wonder, is it worth the effort to construct a whole new life? Are there blueprints to follow? Is there a framework to build on? One moment in time and everything seems to be in ruin – nothing is as it was. Where do I go? What do I do? Who cares? There are so many questions without answers. They all seem to illusively whirl around just out of reach. It feels like hell on earth with the burning searing pain inside that never seems to cease. I seem to be wandering aimlessly in a cloud of sadness and confusion. It is not supposed to be this way. My daughter is supposed to be here to take care of me in my old age. The child is not supposed to die before the parent. Everything seems out of order descending into chaos. "Being aimless is a miserable place to be."[2]

Constructivists talk about the value of rebuilding one's shattered world, but they do not provide blueprints and instructions. Transforming fundamentally how one operates in the world is a major experience. The struggle to make meaning out of confusion and chaos and brokenness may impact psychological and physical well-being.

I had to come to terms with the fact that life was very fragile. I had to learn to live a new life. The outside of my life looked as if it remained the same, but the internal went to war. In the struggle, not one part of my life would escape, not one part could remain untouched by my daughter's death. Life changed. It will never be the same. I can't go back. I'm not sure I want to go forward. I'm stuck in the here and now, the present. "Many studies have shown that the death of one's child causes more stress than any other event that can occur in a person's lifetime."[3]

My friend and longtime mentor, Marjory, came to me with a strong impression from the Lord. She felt that she was to remind me Melanie is not dead in the eternal spiritual sense. The separation is long and painful, but necessary for the special purpose she is filling in serving God. There has been no closure. Closure happens when a task is finished and over, allowing one to walk away without looking back. For three years, I could not allow myself to live in such pain. I was so committed to her memory and keeping up my image. Now, I must give myself permission to grieve and to live in and through the pain. I must release the pain from the secret places of my heart, as it is bearable. She said that it was time to go on, so I began the process of reconstruction.

Still, the struggle continued; I didn't want to adjust to life without my daughter. I didn't want life to go on. She was the focus of my caregiving 24 hours a day for three years and three months. How is it possible to adjust to an empty house and lost days? My whole life revolved around Melanie. Everything I had done for three years and three months had been taken from me! Where would I begin? The central part of my identity was no longer there. My husband had his work; his identity was not lost. My son was far away at college; he had distance, direction and focus. The recurring questions were: Where do I belong? Who needs me? What is my purpose? I asked God to give me the wisdom to know what to do; I asked him to give me the will to do what he wanted me to do. And I asked him to give me the strength to endure the grief experience and not to waste anything. I believe that it is all His to use to bring honor and glory to Himself. This is my belief and the way I responded.

The purpose of grief is to integrate the deceased into your life in a different way. The old view on grief was to break the attachment with the deceased, but a new grief paradigm suggests maintaining connection, but in a different way. We survivors need a revised narrative that allows for meaning in our lives and also in the life of the deceased. This revision process needs active interaction in a community that recognizes the death and mourns the dead, while validating and sharing a continuing bond with them.

Research suggests that there are pathways to choose as individuals process grief. Ruminative coping procures negative moods or thinking; it interferes with behavior and problem solving. Some may shift to more positive thinking simply to get relief from the distress of negative thinking; positive thinking then sustains coping. If we settle into a static positive state, grieving may be neglected. Conversely, if we constantly reside in a negative domain, grief may be intensified. It seems essential that oscillating between negative and positive states allows us to explore multiple dimensions of bereavement. Grieving is something we do organically in all facets and dimensions of our being at once.

This is the way it happened in my life. Once the grief dominated my life, I had to find a way out. "… Experience has suggested that because a child's death is such a significant event, parents' recall of events during the child's illness and at the time of death is likely to remain clear in their minds for long periods of time."[4] Every waking and the few sleeping moments were filled with Melanie. Every detail from the time she was born until she died: the scraped knee, the mashed fingers, every childhood "boo-boo," the sniffles and fevers and upsets of the stomach, they all haunted me, causing me to wonder where I missed out, what I did that was wrong. Did I miss something along the way? Counterfactual thoughts, usually based on "what if" or "if only" concepts, explore "…what one might have done to prevent the event from happening" and may wreck the life of a grieving individual.[5] There is constantly reliving of the details of diagnosis, of going into the treatment room for radiation, soothing the ears that were so deeply burned and sometimes bleeding, covered in the white salve for some degree of relief. She walked through the mall, hair tucked behind ears, obviously white ears, smiling as she talked with my mother, saying, "If someone asks we'll just tell them I'm working on my clown makeup." There are memories of preparing the special foods required by macrobiotics which she sometimes had

31

difficulty eating. It was not easy for a teenager to put aside hamburgers, pizza, macaroni and cheese and fried chicken in exchange for seaweed and nori and adzuki beans and rice. I no longer had any motivation to prepare nutritious satisfying meals for my husband and myself. And the thought of having guests in the house for a meal posed an impossible task. Her school, her room, the pool without a swimmer, the trampoline without a jumper, the cat without a mistress all longed for the return of Melanie. We knew she would not be back. The cognitive level knew, but the affective part still yearned.

Years after the grief has softened and a significant amount of grief work has been done, mothers feel a need to acknowledge their child or children who have died. This phenomenon is not easily understood by those who have not personally experienced the death of one of their children.[6]

"As parents 'move into their grief,' the complexity of their bond with the child becomes expressed in the complexity of their grief."[7] Every aspect of life may be affected by the loss, including work. If work serves as a distraction, an opportunity to have some sense of familiarity and routine, then it is not unusual to be overwhelmed with strong emotions as the transition is made into the "at home" time. Some parents are unable to work due to the intensity of grief.

Grief challenges the "assumptive world." The assumptive world is what one becomes so accustomed to in life that it may be taken for granted until challenged by some life event. It includes patterns of life and habits of life, interaction with people and places. Simply, it is the life and space one lives and operates in daily. "Bereavement shatters our taken-for-granted life patterns and undermines many of our life assumptions."[8] And yet "our fundamental assumptions are the bedrock of our conceptual system; they are the assumptions that we are least aware of and least likely to challenge."[9]

There needs to be an understanding of bereavement that acknowledges the need for revising the assumptive world, the meaning system and the life narrative. Acknowledging and appreciating grief as a process that reconstructs the world of meaning and restores coherence to a person's narrative might influence the attitude and understanding toward bereavement. Bereavement changes the world in such a way that the world as one knew it no longer exists.

The lostness of grief feels strange, somewhat like wandering around inside a brown paper bag. Somehow you know there was an entrance, but you wonder if there will ever be an exit. Some grieving individuals continually seek to find the meaning or purpose of a loss or trauma event. The aimless wandering, the weaving, the searching, the sense of looking for something, but not knowing where to look, all gave me a sense of helplessness. It is not unusual for bereaved mothers to feel a sense of helplessness or hopelessness. Going room to room walking, moving as if in slow motion, weaving and wandering, wondering where to look and what to look for, sometimes unaware of retracing the same steps over and over, I paced. It was the same everywhere – nothingness.

The coffee is made, but who shares it with me? There is so much that needs to be done, but who does it with me? Social disruption prompted me to wonder if I had a place, and event disruption caused me to question the order of life. "...These dual disruptions are the most difficult traumas to transcend – the most difficult to turn into growth."[10]

What is the use? What is the point anyway? Who cares? Now that it is over...but is it over? Is it ever over? What am I? Who am I? Do I have a purpose? It seems imperative to make meaning of this profound loss. My career of caring for Melanie was over. Where do I go from here? My job is over, but does that mean I cease to be? What, now, is my purpose? How do I fill my empty days: Sleep them away? There is no sleep. It does not come. Work the days away? Doing what, cleaning the house or straightening the closets? Oh, what does it matter? Who cares anyway? Traumatic stress shatters our core assumptions of the world.

Your Turn

What intentional action are you prompted to take to reconstruct your life?

Write, draw, or doodle your thoughts here.

THE INTENTIONAL ACTION
OF
RELEARNING MY WORLD

It seems God let us down. I wonder why he didn't respond in the way we anticipated. I didn't want it. I didn't like it. I was angry with God. I thought he let us down. I also felt he let the faith community down. The biblical character Job sat against a religious system, and so did I. Part of me still says this should not have happened. "Spiritually, we seek peace and consolation. We modify our hopes and deepen or modify our faiths."[11] Some individuals may feel comforted by their faith and others may feel abandoned by their faith.

One revealing experience was related to cold weather and Melanie. She became easily chilled, resulting in muscle contractions that then led to muscle aches, pains and discomfort. On a cold winter day I had a chiropractic appointment. As I prepared for treatment I realized I had layer upon layer upon layer of clothing topped by a very heavy coat, and I gained an awareness of dressing like Melanie dressed for protection against the cold. The wise doctor, who did not know Melanie, engaged me in conversation allowing me time, as I tried to verbally make meaning from the symbolic actions. As the doctor worked with my body, some emotions characteristic of grief began to emerge. I felt a sense of anger that she was gone, guilt that I had not kept her warm enough, fear that I could not control emotions, and helplessness when I could not control the overwhelming tears. No excuses were necessary and I was too drained to apologize for the uncharacteristic behavior. He created a safe haven with soothing music, leaving an assistant to be with me as I rested to regain strength, energy and focus before driving home. They were patient and kind as I remained there well into the afternoon. This defining connection reestablishing relationship at a point of Melanie's pain was the beginning of my awareness of the layers and complexity of my grief. Reflectively this was my initial sense that I had a lot of work to do, peeling layer after layer, much like the clothing or like the many layers of an onion. Characteristic of some onions, peeling the layers brings tears even though the taste is sweet.

Struggling with loss and grief, and struggling with life after loss, in a process called relearning the world, both seem to characterize life for bereaved individuals. Relearning our world as we learn to live with grief, we tend to move in different directions simultaneously. "…We return to aspects of our lives that are still viable…and…we transform ourselves as we reshape and redirect our individual, family, and community lives."[12]

Being intentional about relearning the world, within the context of grief, in an effort to make meaning from the loss of a loved one, requires initiative and action in a conscious search for something good from a painful, hard experience. On the other hand, finding meaning throughout the bereavement period suggests the realization of an unconscious "knowing" and appreciation while suffering. "Relearning the world after someone we love has died is not a matter of taking in information or mastering ideas or theories. It is, rather, a matter of learning again *how to be and act in the world* without those we love by our sides."[13]

My son lost not only his sister, but also his parents for a time. "It is common for siblings of the lost child to be overlooked during the time immediately following the death."[14]

I had to relearn how to be a wife, how to focus on the needs of my husband, how to be a mother to my son, how to plan and prepare meals, how to exercise and consider self-care. I gained 20 pounds of weight the first year of bereavement. I also had to relearn how to be in the house alone, how to be a friend and to have friends in an atmosphere of fun. I had to seek ways to find balance in every aspect of my life. I had to relearn my personal world in such a way that I cared if I lived or died.

Some people adapt to new circumstances and a changed world more readily than others. Some people adapt slowly, stumbling, floundering and sometimes getting "stuck" in the on-going process of grief. When people are unable to articulate or express the pain of grief, it may be helpful to engage a counselor, therapist and/or bereavement facilitator.

Counselors or therapists may need to show us other paths through suggestive stories about how others have found their way through these transitions or they teach us to be more self-reflective and deliberate in making rather than simply discovering meaning as we change.[15]

I needed a miracle of my own. I needed the will to live my life. I needed to find the strength. I needed something to fight for – so I could hang on. It seemed like a nightmare that would never end – day after day, the empty house, the empty hours, the empty arms, the empty life. I needed something new, something entirely different. I needed to be reborn to find a new perspective on life. The death of our daughter destroyed my self-confidence and almost destroyed my desire to live. Doubts, misgivings and questions plagued me. I could do nothing acceptable or worthwhile in my own estimation. I kept doing and doing at a faster and faster pace just to keep from disappearing into despair. I had a need for approval, to feel loved and accepted. I needed security and comfort and a foundation where I could plant my feet.

A paradox in my social construct was that I had to give up control to regain control. There was control of emotions, control of life, but the confusion in my mind was tearing me apart. I was too hurt to cry and tried to mediate the hurt by meditation. Meditation is the art of quieting thoughts and calming the spirit with a focus on breath control; it is a centuries-old technique that can reduce stress and lower blood pressure,

41

restoring a sense of peace and balance. I meditated by: repeating Psalm 23; walking with awareness of every step, every bird, every flower; being mindful of every house in the neighborhood and praying for each resident with a forced, systematic focus.

Established and expected ways of grieving may not be totally satisfactory for us; therefore, "…we may need to make new ways that work for us…We relearn in all dimensions of our lives. As we do, we relearn ourselves. Emotionally, we temper the pain of our suffering. Psychologically, we renew our self-confidence, self-esteem, and self-identity. Behaviorally, we transform our habits, motivations, dispositions, ways of doing things." Often there is a need for change; the old ways of doing things no longer seem to fit. "…We spontaneously try alternative ways of being and acting and find that some work for us."[16]

At a graduate level seminar on the psychology of appreciation, the focus was on the power of appreciating daily "happenings," in essence, learning to celebrate the small things as well as the more evident big things. This learning experience affirmed the attitude we adopted with Melanie when we intentionally made even the mundane task of going to the grocery store an adventure. Our focus was not on the products purchased, but rather on the act of shopping.

"We can choose when and where we approach what affects us most."[17] There may be times we can go into areas frequented by the one who died and then again there may be times when we feel that the overwhelming surge of pain is more than we can bear. The first time I went shopping without Melanie, I chose a new recently built mall. I thought since we had not shopped that site together there would be no memories of her in that place. The shop windows were dressed with the colors of autumn, the browns, greens, oranges, beige, and off-white that Melanie wore so well. Melanie was everywhere, yet she was nowhere. I was totally unprepared for the volcano of soul pain that simmered. There was urgency, a sense to run, run far away and escape the colors of Melanie. I made a decision, a choice, to stay: to stay and embrace the pain. Methodically and purposefully I walked every section in slow measured steps, passing every store window in the entire mall, fastening my gaze straight ahead, avoiding the colors that filled the windows, seeing, but not seeing through a blur of tears. Returning to my car there was a triumphant feeling that quickly melted into erupting sobs. Through the tears I caught a glimpse of a yellow butterfly playing around the windshield of my car. The choice is to advance or retreat, avoiding the familiar, until we feel able to deal with the pain of the place alone or in the company of someone else.[18] We lose more than the person who died, we may also lose the joy of going to places or doing things the deceased enjoyed. Friends had offered their service in any encounter. I was appreciative, but no, no, she was mine. I wanted to hold her to myself even in her absence.

She was no longer dancing through the house filling it with laughter, chatter and love. I could not stay hour upon hour inside the house. It seemed that the school hours were tolerable, but about the time school was out, I needed to be out and about. But there was nowhere to go – no dancing classes, no church activities, no friends to visit, and no homework. Her room was empty. Her space at the table was empty. We had a car without a driver, a pool without a swimmer. Her space on the church pew at Sunday morning worship service was empty.

"In grieving we must relearn our very selves, including our characters, histories and roles, and identities that we find in them. We must also relearn our self-confidence and self-esteem."[19]

Your Turn

What intentional action are you prompted to take to relearn your world?

Write, draw, or doodle your thoughts here.

THE INTENTIONAL ACTION
OF
REESTABLISHING RELATIONSHPS

I found myself with a package I did not ask for. And I wondered, as C.S. Lewis did after the death of his beloved wife Joy, What am I going to do with the package? Life is constantly filled with choices. All of our relationships are challenged, from the most intimate to the casual acquaintances. We consider the meaning of relationships both in the context of life with the one who died and life now after the person's death. We wonder if preexisting relationships still have meaning and if new relationships will be affected by the life and death of the one who died. We wonder who will be comfortable interacting with us and who will shift away from us. We might question, "'About whom will we continue or come to care?' ...In grieving we relearn our relationships with those who died."[20]

47

"…Bereaved persons struggle to articulate a changed sense of self and to find validation for it in both real and symbolically significant bonds with other people."[21]

When someone becomes a memory, that memory becomes a treasure. When major life transitions occur it is not unusual for friends and acquaintances to treat one differently. "That society is significantly threatened and impacted by the loss of a child is evidenced by the manner in which it treats bereaved parents and the unhealthy and inappropriate expectations it maintains and enforces for them."[22] Often acquaintances, friends and even other family members do not know how to relate and be comfortable in the presence of the one who has suffered the loss. They may retreat and ignore or reject former relationships with the bereaved. "In a society that values attractiveness, youth, and productivity, the death of a child, who embodies these attributes, is particularly repugnant."[23]

Just as grief is not experienced as a solitary entity, so life is not a solitary entity. T. Attig states the following:

"Interaction with others profoundly affects our individual relearning...together with others, we reshape and redirect our family and community life patterns and life histories.... We grieve not only as individuals but also as families and communities. We receive and give support and comfort. We depend on one another or make demands."[24]

Researchers have studied social support as a buffer for grief. The support of family, friends, faith communities and other social networks may serve as a buffer against anxiety, depression and/or stress.

"Within all cultures throughout history there has been a support system for persons in grief. The support system contains four basic elements: a close-knit family unit; a caring community of friends and neighbors...; a deep-rooted philosophical or religious attitude toward death; and the continuity and stability provided by known and repeated ceremonial forms and rituals. The full resources of these basic elements are needed for bereaved parents. But these elements of the grief support system cannot be stereotyped or rigid in their application."[25]

In my own experience, the task of restoring equilibrium, of seeking peace or inner harmony, and self-validating activities – it all seemed so senseless. I needed someone to tell me I was a good mother, that I had done everything humanly possible to save my daughter's life. I needed my motherhood validated. I needed new relationships. I needed to rediscover how to self-validate in my changed life. I needed something to strengthen my resolve, efforts and methods of validation. The realization of the fragility of life caused me to live every moment as if it may be the last. "We find affirmation for our self-narratives in the responses of significant others, our sense of identity is strained, and sometimes sundered, by the loss of these relationships."[26]

Sleeplessness and stress of grief contributed to panic attacks and a sense of being watched or followed, and claustrophobic tendencies heightened. To get over my fears they had to be faced – faced and embraced. Two years after Melanie's death, I was still smiling and saying, "I'm fine, thank you," whenever I was asked how I was. Late one afternoon, Melanie's doctor from Duke called to say that we had been on his mind. He was calling to inquire about how things were going with us. "Just fine," I said. "My husband is into his work schedule and I am getting back into some of my activities. We are all right. All is going well." Hanging up after the brief conversation and walking out of the study into the hallway, I felt as if I had been drenched by a bucket of ice-cold water with the sudden realization, that, indeed, I was not fine. My daughter had died, my life was different, my world was turned upside down and I was not fine. Immediately, I called the doctor's pager. As I waited for him to respond, there was the revelation, the first real awareness that life was not as it should be. There seemed to be a strong need to admit to someone that I was living a pretend existence, and life was not peaches and cream. When the phone rang, I answered. The doctor asked, "What's up?" I admitted, "I lied to you. I am not fine. My daughter died, and I am not fine." Then he asked, "Whom are you talking to?" Not understanding the meaning of the question, I asked, "What do you mean?" "Whom are you talking to about Melanie's death? About what you are feeling? About the whole situation?" clarified the doctor. "I'm not feeling much of anything. And I'm not talking to anyone." "What about your church? I thought you were receiving a lot of support from your church. Isn't there someone there you can talk to? You've got to talk. Unless you start talking, healing will never begin. You've got to find someone to talk with.

If you can't find someone there, let me know, I will find someone for you. It is very important; you must find someone to talk with." Then he told me his personal grief story that originated in his childhood. There had been no talking and no reconciliation or resolution until adulthood, after the loss of a significant relationship, a remarriage, and birth of children; then the impact of grief began to play havoc in his life again. Trained professionals helped him see that current issues were related to unresolved grief issues. Confident that life would be healthier for me, he insisted that I begin talking and periodically update him on the progress. He reiterated over and over, "You have got to talk and talk and talk."

But I felt there was no one. The church seemed the logical place for me, but there had been a turnover of ministerial staff and leadership. As large as our faith community was, I did not feel there was anyone I could talk with. They were new, and didn't even know Melanie. I felt very isolated and alone even around people I had known for years. I think somewhere deep inside, I knew talking would be necessary, but locating someone seemed like a task too large to tackle. I felt as if I were marking time until a trusted and experienced person could be engaged. The willpower for this cannot be taught. It must come from within, finding the courage to journey deep into the soul. I made an effort to locate someone I felt comfortable would honor my daughter's memory and hear me out, but there was so much hurt and anger inside me that I was unwilling or unable to settle on one person. Actually, as is sometimes the case, I was consciously unaware of the existence of internal anger and would have been unwilling to admit it if I had been aware. After all, who or what would be the object and how could a "prim and proper" Southern belle admit and express such strong emotion? As I interviewed prospective counselors, I continuously found one reason or another why each was not the right one. It seemed there was always something that irritated me. Little did I know that the irritation was my own sandpaper brushing against another's personality. There seemed to be a fire burning in my soul that required me to find some meaning in the entire experience, that some way somehow I must make some sense of it all. There was a crisis of faith in my belief system and my value system. There seemed to me an innate knowledge that my counselor, my sounding board must be someone firmly grounded and planted in Christian views, values and traditions. I needed someone who could listen and not be offended. I needed someone who would allow me to talk, sorting out strong feelings without judgment. I needed someone who could assure me that it was all right to be angry, that God was big enough not only to handle my anger, but also to invite me to empty it out. As is often the case, I could see evidence of anger in my husband, but not in myself. I had to search for meaning and reasons to continue living.

    Friends who watched our daughter grow up and interface with their own children were grieving for the loss of Melanie. They found it difficult to talk about our loss and we found it somewhat difficult to continue the relationship as it had been. We no longer needed our meals prepared, porch swept, or laundry done by them. Life had drastically changed for us; it seemed that we no longer knew how to converse. We were always aware of their foundational support, but it seemed we all needed some distance. Over time awareness of appreciation for the depth of the relationships has returned with the assurance that we are not resentful that their sons and daughters are healthy and have enriched life with children of their own. Many of our friends did not know what to say. They wanted to help, to make things better, but no one knew how. Neither did I. We needed some new people in our lives, people who would let us talk about Melanie. Over time our circle of influence has been extended to include new relationships. In a time of grief it seems so unfair that the burden of seeking new relationships rests with the bereaved.

In my grief, I began to recognize the unique and special nature of another community to which I now belong: the community of those who suffer from the pain of grief over the diagnosis and loss of a child. I now saw things differently. Life had a deeper meaning. I needed contact with others who understood the depth of the suffering and pain, but would also offer support and encouragement. I attended an informal support group of mothers who had experienced the death of a child. My loss was fresh and raw, but it seemed they could only dwell on their own past losses. I left feeling as if I was the consoler and they were the consoled. Weeks passed before I tried again, but it was a repeat of the previous experience with the small group of mothers. Leaving the second time, I prayed, Lord, please do not send me there again. In my perception, these women used the group in unhealthy ways to continuously seek sympathy, without forward movement, as a means of adjustment.

Bereavement is a difficult journey. "Many studies have shown that the death of one's child causes more stress than any other event that can occur in a person's lifetime."[27] My sisters had their children; my friends had their children. I made a conscious choice to face grief and to embrace the pain in an effort to be a participant in the lives of my nieces and nephews, Melanie's friends and other young women who might enter my life. Over time, in spite of the pain or perhaps because of it, some deep relationships have formed with young women and young men. Intentional decisions must be made by people in the grief process to continue or reestablish relationships in spite of the painful memories. "In the wake of bereavement, then, we are forced to renegotiate our identity as a survivor in interaction with others, seeking an audience that will validate the new version of self we enact."[28]

Superficial politeness and shallow conversation was irritating. Wearing masks and keeping a guard up were additional defenses that discouraged the establishment of meaningful relationships. It was my intentional decision to reestablish relationships with those who separated themselves from us because they did not want to open themselves to the pain. Well-intentioned people may at times speak words that cut deeply or spark irritation. My theory is they did not set out to inflict additional pain. They did not know appropriate healing words to speak; therefore, it has become my practice to grace well-intentioned people and hope others will grace me when my comments sting. In the process of grieving, an individual may experience a loss of support and friendships, but conversely they may also experience a strengthening of relationships and even the establishment of new friendships. Bereaved persons may exhibit more concern for others, a higher value on relationships, and an increased openness.

Engaging in creative expressive behaviors has connected me with people I would otherwise not have known. Participating in an Institute for Care at End of Life, sponsored jointly by Duke University Divinity School and Duke University Medical Center, and relating to the use of music in end of life care, I made a new acquaintance who shared some common experiences and interests. This acquaintance, who is proficient in drumming, teaches the use of drumming as a means of stress release and healing. This has developed into a professional and personal relationship that was the beginning of my meeting a team of academic and clinical expressive arts professionals at an Institute for Expressive Arts at Appalachian State University

Establishing these new relationships extended my opportunity for networking and for developing additional relationships.

In the bereaved social world one often needs permission to share his or her story of loss. Sharing the pain of loss with the bereaved is often referred to as "being there." In reference to the death of a child, "'being there' means being with the parent in a way that acknowledges that the reality of the child's death and the reality of the pain are not the parent's alone."[29] It is often said that those who have the greatest understanding of the pain of loss are others who have also experienced the death of a child because they have "been there."

"We also grieve in interaction with those who enter our lives after the death. Some take peripheral places, some central. Some present new challenges. Some prove to be sources of new support. They may or may not be welcome additions to our families or communities."[30]

Helen, Caryl and Karen are all members of my same faith community, but I had never met them until a crisis event of death came into each one's life. Helen's 16-year-old son was tragically killed in an automobile accident. He was not a contributor to the accident; his vehicle was stationary at a stop sign when an 18-wheel truck slammed into him. Now, Helen has been trained as a lay caregiver, readily reaching out to others. Caryl's 29-year-old son checked himself into a hospital with back pain one Friday. In less than two weeks she planned his funeral. Over time, in the process of an extended formal caring relationship, she began to sense an urging to read the obituary section of the daily newspaper. When she reads about the death of a son, she contacts the mother, often writing a note and sending a copy of the grief survival card I authored. Karen's nine-month-old niece, who lived out-of-state, was diagnosed with a brain stem tumor. Through her daughter's first grade teacher she learned about our experience with Melanie. The teacher, a long-time family friend, knew Melanie intimately. The teacher was the mediator who spoke the truth in love, provided support, encouragement and comfort. Karen's niece died five years ago. I was unaware of this situation until February 2004. Karen's name and phone number were handed to me with the suggestion that she might enjoy working on a special collaborative project for our church. Introducing myself in a telephone conversation, she spoke my name several times, then she asked some questions establishing a connection before she asked, "Do you have a daughter named Melanie?" I affirmed her query, after which she related the story of her niece. With emotion evident in the sound of her voice, she expressed gratitude, commenting that I had helped her and her extended family process the grief from her niece. I was a stranger to the situation until that moment. We made arrangements for a face-to-face introduction. Overwhelmed, she commented that she always wanted to say thank you to me, but never dreamed that she would have the opportunity. This is just a small sampling of the way new people come into my life. God has not put me with a bereavement group, but he has sprinkled my life full of bereaved individuals. Within the past two weeks, I have participated with six separate newly bereaved families, primarily women.

The first springtime after Melanie's death, we invited a group of Melanie's girlfriends to share a mountain retreat weekend. They freely talked about Melanie and experiences they shared. Opening my retreat space to this group of girls was a leap for me. My husband delighted in having frequent contact with her friends; they were a sense of comfort for him. For me, knowingly there was a sense of resistance because they filled my daughter's space and it was difficult.

It is important to disclose personal stories as a way of connecting with people and being understood. People want to share their insights into life. Talking is important, but listening is supreme. Sometimes reaching out to touch a hand or shoulder is all that is necessary. "Baring one's soul through the common pain of grief is the cement for many friendships. Closer relationships with select people seem to be a relatively common result of losing a loved one."[31]

Death changes family structure. If families talk about the loss, and how responsibilities and roles may shift because of it, they seem to gain more satisfaction in making meaning of the loss. When families talk they seek to create some sort of order in the disorderliness of death, and seek to gain some control over the natural phenomenon of death. Whereas, a "no talk about it family" sometimes delays grief expression, and the process of family meaning making may be inhibited. If family relationships are fragile or if there is a sense of protectiveness of family secrets, then families may be closed to engaging in meaning making with others.

"Loss typically produces significant distress for most people, and the greater facility in self-disclosure, coupled with a desire to share one's own experience, can lead to a kind of 'empathy training,' allowing survivors of loss a chance to become more closely connected to significant others."[32]

The concept of retaining a strong relationship while loving in absence is familiar: my husband goes to work, and I love him though I do not see him. My son, pursuing his medical career in another state, is my heartstring, not my apron string. I do not see him or his wife often, yet I know love transcends time and distance. My Mother, the woman who gave me life and poured her life into her family, lives two hours driving distance, yet I know without a doubt that her love for me continues and will forever. Why, then, I wonder, does it seem so strange to some that bone of my bone and flesh of my flesh, my daughter, will forever hold her sacred place of love in my life even though her physical presence is not available to me?

Mothers and fathers may reestablish relationships in different means. Parents who have lost a child may grieve differently, having needs that seem to be soothed by opposite poles. If parents live within themselves, with no communication about grief, the sense of understanding and being understood diminishes. Historically women value open communication more than men. Two researchers who explored grief communication, reactions and marital satisfaction in bereaved parents discovered that attitudes about communication and grief shifted over time. They found the level of communication influenced the nature of the change. Expressing emotions and self-disclosure seem to contribute to a positive sense of well-being in those who have experienced undesirable circumstances in life. Other researchers indicate "...Self-disclosure can provide an opportunity for an individual to try out new behaviors with appropriate people in his or her support system."[33]

It is not unusual for marriages to experience relationship conflict in the adjustment to bereavement. The quality of the relationship prior to bereavement regarding unresolved emotions of the past may impact adjustment to loss. Blame of self or the other may result if the bereaved perceive failure in living up to expectations or have remorse of past actions. Some marriages drifted apart and ended after the couples "were unable to console each other, each being deep into his or her own grief."[34] Severe marital conflict may arise during the illness or after the death of a child. Undercurrents of anger, guilt, blame or resentment may be manifested in behaviors and/or attitudes of one or both parents. "Not only must we struggle to let go of their physical presence and longing for their return, but we also need to let go of any singular, sometimes preoccupying, focus on them and their absence. We need to let go of loving only them to the exclusion of any others."[35]

Strong winds blow, often demolishing marriage, especially if it was shaky. Some clean up the inward house, but do not clean up the marriage. We made an intentional choice to salvage our marriage relationship. The nuclear family and faith family survived. I was keenly aware that life was forever changed. For three years the full focus of life was on Melanie. As we left the hospital in the dawn of a new day, turning from the exit ramp of the parking lot onto the highway, I looked up and saw the full moon, so huge it beckoned me to reach up and touch it, and I sensed my daughter's presence. "Hey, Van, look! That is a Melanie moon. Hey, Melanie!" We entered a day we had not anticipated and did not want. As my husband and I rounded the exit ramp from the interstate, I turned toward him as he drove in silence and said, "We now have a choice to make. So many marriages end in divorce after the illness and/or death of a child.

The statistics are not in our favor. We must decide if we are going to allow this to drive a wedge between us to separate us or if it is going to draw us together cementing us even more closely together. We have a son; we must remember him, also. Melanie's death can make us or break us." My husband said, "For me that is easy. I have just lost my daughter; I don't want to lose my wife also."

We knew the statistics. An overwhelmingly high percentage of couples that lost a child or faced tragic illness also faced divorce. We had faced statistics before: only five percent of patients had Melanie's type of cancer. None had survived. We were going to be the one exception to that grim forecast, we thought. We did not have to succumb to the present statistical forecast. Our marriage would not fall victim to this threat. Then and there, before we ever even arrived home from the hospital after Melanie's death, we reaffirmed our commitment to each other and to God to do whatever was necessary to relearn our world and rebuild our lives, remaining true to our marriage relationship. It was not an easy road to travel. In the onslaught and aftermath of the emptiness, the pain, the sorrow and suffering, it would have been easy to turn our backs to each other in blame, anger, defeat or a myriad of other possibilities.

"...Parents experience loss upon loss. ...Closeness that characterizes the marital relationship and usually provides its greatest strength can be a disadvantage in this case, as it makes partners particularly vulnerable to the feelings of blame and anger grievers often displace onto those nearest to them."[36]

Remembering our marriage vows, the commitment to each other and before God, we worked to rekindle the love relationship between us. Now, 23 years after her death, we still work at maintaining closeness. We have learned that love is an action, not feelings. What is important to me is important to him and conversely, what is important to him is important to me, because we consciously make it that way. I put forth effort to meet his needs and he does the same for me. We had to learn to communicate all over again verbally and physically. "Sexual abstinence is frequently reported by couples due to a lack of sexual interest because of overwhelming grief. The opposite can also be true. Sexual activity may be sought out by some couples shortly after the death."[37] At times, I have been very unlovable, and at times, he has been very unlovable. Those are the times we often need to be loved the most. We clung to our promises to each other and to God's Word. We also remembered the poet

Rumi's view, "Where there is ruin, there is hope for treasure."

One's belief system, though initially shaken, may grow stronger in the process of struggling with grief. Spiritual beliefs and the support of a faith community may contribute to finding comfort in sorrow and new meaning in life. In a research project with 300 adults who had lost a loved one, an overwhelming majority "said that their religious and spiritual beliefs helped them during their grief,"[38] but in some cases, religious and spiritual beliefs are broken and need to be reestablished. Some people turn "away from previously held religious beliefs because of the inability to make religious sense of their loss."[39]

> "…With their hurt, pain, and anger, the bereaved parents will search for answers to the age-old questions of the philosophical and religious meaning of life and of death. No matter what the religious background of the parents, it appears that most, if not all, seek support from religious sources."[40]

One researcher indicated religion shifted from formal to personal, with some mothers questioning God but ending with a strengthened faith, realizing God was all they had and all they really needed.

The Biblical character Job's friends came to comfort him in the face of human suffering, but they tried to rationalize and justify his suffering. Job held on to his integrity, refusing to succumb to their condemnation. He did not deserve what had happened to him; neither did I. Melanie's death was not some cruel punishment from a God who demands such retribution. God was present in our suffering. He sustains us in a fallen world that suffers disease and the death of the innocent. The Old Testament biblical character Job did not give up on God. Neither did I.

In my spiritual tradition, establishing relationship with God and believing in life after death promotes continuing bonds with Melanie, building lasting love in a reshaped relationship.[41]

Your Turn

What intentional action are you prompted to take to reestablish your relationships?

Write, draw, or doodle your thoughts here.

ETHEREAL DANCER

Our beautiful daughter, Melanie, died in August, 1990, of an inoperable brain tumor. One Monday afternoon a few weeks after her death, I walked outside in the backyard, missing her terribly, as I relived the happy, playful days of her seventeen years with us. I felt that my heart would burst if I could not get some relief from the grief and pain.

I looked up at the sky, remembering how often Melanie and I searched for cloud shapes. As my eyes lifted, so did my heart, for there in the bright blue sky above me, I saw one single cloud.

Suddenly I heard Melanie's voice inside me, calling, "Look, Mom! I'm dancing! I'm dancing, Mom! I'm free. I'm dancing and I'm free!"

The peach cloud above me formed a lively, graceful dancer, with widespread arms and long leaping legs.

I gazed up, letting my eyes drink in the beauty of the dancer, then I raced to the telephone to call a friend. It was 5:30 in the afternoon. I could not reach my friend or my husband. I snatched up my camera to capture "dancing Melanie," as I called my cloud-vision.

Two weeks later my mother came to visit me. She told me of a fascinating experience she had late one Monday afternoon as she drove her car toward her home, two hours away from our city. Suddenly she noticed a vivid peach cloud formation in an otherwise cloudless sky. She described it as a leaping figure, with full flowing skirts and long arms out flung into the sky above her. She hesitated, then asked carefully, "Maybe an...angel?" I looked at her and said quietly, "Could it have been a dancer?"

"Oh, yes, yes! A dancer! A Melanie dancer!"

We had prayed that Melanie would be free to run and jump and leap and dance when she was wholly restored. And she can! God allowed Melanie's mother and grandmother to see her in the act, even to get a picture of her "leaping across the sky."

Dee G.
Nov. 4, 1990

"Look Mom, I'm dancing! I'm dancing and I'm free."

THE INTENTIONAL ACTION
OF
REBIRTHING A PLACE FOR
MELANIE

Ritual, closing, and separation ceremonies help us begin remembering even as we plan and participate in those activities that help us say goodbye to the physical life. Perhaps we say goodbye to the physical as we say hello to remembering. Perhaps that is the beginning of moving from a relationship of physical presence to a relationship of physical absence with a transition of memory. "Grief is always about a minimum of two people: the one who is grieving and the one who is lost."[42] When family members talk about a loss, struggling to make some sense of it, they attach meaning to the absence of the deceased.

73

I want to remember, never to forget Melanie. I must find ways to ensure her memory continues, as does the impact of her life. I never want to stop loving her and I resist those who try to say that I must let all facets of her go. "The central challenge as we grieve is moving from a life where we loved them in presence to a new life where we love them in absence. Nothing is more difficult. Nothing is more important. Nothing is more rewarding... We want to keep loving them, but don't know how."[43] There must be some way to make this transition to memory and lasting love in absence. What I carry in my heart that represents Melanie must be translated into outward acts as a continuing connection is maintained. "The goal of grief is not to sever the bond with the dead child but to integrate the child into the parent's life and social networks in a different way than when the child was alive."[44]

My quest then became ways to remember Melanie. The first Christmas without her, rather than our usual party for our friends, we focused on the friends of our children. We planned a party to bring the friends together in our home.

When family Christmas gifts are exchanged at my Mother's house Melanie is included. Even though I was numb that first Christmas, in the space that was Melanie's turn, as we usually open gifts in age order, I shared a card in her memory and gave everyone a photograph of her. In Melanie's time and space for receiving, we gave. Giving typified her life.

Now we, my husband and I, give to family members and close friends a yearly calendar adorned with a photograph of Melanie. They usually display the calendar on their refrigerator or some other prominent place, honoring her memory. Often family members give us a "remembering Melanie" gift. Over the years gifts have included ornaments for the Christmas tree, books, bells, angel figurines, candles, angel lights, music boxes with reminders of a dancer or an angel, among other things. My Mother stamps her card designs with "Melanie's Memories by MeMa." Many feel comfortable with linking objects as a means of connecting with the dead child. Another method of connection is linking objects, which may include jewelry, clothing, special books or other strong reminders of the child. Melanie's name is also linked to sunsets and rainbows, mountaintops and ocean shores. Parents may feel validated when they are given the opportunity to talk about the linking object, describing its significance. Sharing pain creates bonds and may create community.

The first springtime without Melanie, the article written by her, "God In My Life," with an accompanying photograph, was published in *Discipleship Training Magazine.* We have shared copies of this article literally all over the world. We usually do not leave home without copies of the article in the trunk of the car, in a briefcase, or even tucked into my purse. Sharing meanings with others seems to enhance the process of meaning making. If I feel accepted, understood, and supported, then it may be easier to process grief and adjust Melanie from a place of presence to a place of memory.

Practical legacies are a means of being connected to those we love. This may include possessions, projects and promises. Material resources may continue to provide for survivors, projects the loved one sponsored may receive continuing investments of resources that include time and/or finances, and promises made to the loved one or by the deceased loved one may be fulfilled. Melanie wanted to attend the New York premiere of the Randy James DanceWorks Company; we were present at the performance in her absence. Specific ways of doing things may be maintained: when my daughter's room is cleaned, it still is important to me to return her miniature perfume bottles to the exact location chosen by her. Perhaps this is influenced by the memory of her distress when she returned from school one day to discover that when someone cleaned her room the miniature collection had been replaced randomly. Melanie did not get angry often, but on this particular occasion she allowed us to know of her great displeasure.

Neither is it unusual to develop an interest in or begin to support areas of interest of the deceased. My husband and I have developed a tender spot for young female dancers, particularly dancers at Columbia College, Columbia, South Carolina. We find ourselves in the bittersweet arena of attending concerts and sometimes interacting with student dancers. Celebrating traditions appreciated by our deceased loved ones also seems to connect us with them.

Soulful legacies include things the deceased taught survivors about: "…ways of caring about, and loving, things, places, food, music, ourselves, others, and our families and communities. We make meaning when we deliberately cultivate traditions…we failed to appreciate while they were alive."[45]

Rebirthing Melanie in memory, we have established the tradition of placing flowers in the Riverland Hills Baptist Church worship center on the Sunday preceding her birthday, which is July 28, 1973. At Christmas, she is remembered with poinsettias, and at Easter, with Easter lilies in the church.

A remembrance tree planted near the brain tumor clinic at Duke University Medical Center was nourished by Melanie's name on a piece of paper placed in the prepared hole.

In addition, we donated inscribed memory bricks in the Leadership Walk at Columbia College to honor Melanie and people who impacted her life. Melanie's youthfulness did not negate the appreciation for her dancing ability and spirit. Before the brain tumor diagnosis, she was selected to study dance at Tri-Dac, the Tri-District Arts Consortium for creatively gifted students. Also, she had been offered a dance scholarship at Columbia College. Her death happened one month and one day after her seventeenth birthday, at the beginning of her senior year in high school.

Obviously, she was unable to collect on the proffered scholarship. Seizing the opportunity to create a memory in perpetuity, selected college faculty, administration and staff collaborated with us in planning an event in celebration of the arts. Celebrating the arts on the Sunday afternoon of Melanie's 18th birthday was another way of creating memories. Artists representing dance, music, storytelling, drama, visual and tactile arts created a memorable event with contributions, gifts and donations establishing The Melanie Delores Gulledge Endowed Scholarship. This is yet another example of how Melanie was unable to receive, but she continues to give. The scholarship is awarded annually to a dance major. Libby Patenadue, chairperson of the dance department at that time, and I designed a unique procedure for selection of the recipient. The scholarship is not need-based, but based on character, integrity, spirit, service and compassion. Each spring the dance majors are called together to hear about the uniqueness of the person of Melanie. Several dance faculty members instructed Melanie and understand and retain a high regard for the essence of her. By secret ballot, the dance majors vote on a peer who most nearly exemplifies the qualities of Melanie. I have never been present at this ritual, but I have heard from faculty and students that it is a tender time.

Storytelling and dream-telling are useful methods for meaning making. As stories and/or dreams are told that relate to the deceased, meaning may be revealed. One neighbor recently related a story to me involving the care of her critically sick husband. Often she is awake and up several times in the night caring for him. From her house she can see the continuously burning light in the side window of Melanie's room. According to her, many nights she has drawn strength, courage and hope from seeing the soft glow of the electric candlelight. It seems that nothing is wasted, no matter how small and seemingly insignificant, if it has been dedicated to God to use for His purpose.

In our culture, it is customary to mark the gravesite with the name of the deceased. To be worthy of commemorating Melanie, I felt the marker required special attention. Through the two-year process of researching contractors, stones, and placement of markers by studying, interviewing, visiting cemeteries in North America and Europe, and hearing the stories of others, the design and installation of the monument was completed. Her gravesite is located at the church of my childhood, two hours from our current residence; the monument was specially designed to characterize Melanie's creative life. Black granite is in the shape of an artist palette with a bronze, dancing silhouette of Melanie on one side, with her full name and birth and death dates. The foundation stone has these words: "I'm dancing and I'm free." On the reverse side there is a painted cameo-like image of her with the following three phrases: "pure, holy, and virginal," "a joy to all who knew her," "a special gift of love." The names of her parents and brother are also on that side. Her footstone bears the biblical scripture verse from Habakkuk 3:19, "The Lord God is my strength. He makes my feet like hinds feet and makes me walk on my high places." Mirror polished coping creates the perimeter with the initial "G" etched in gold leaf marking the entirety of the burial plot.

Family and close friends attended a private formal dedication ceremony.

The site location and placement is significant because the foot of Melanie's grave is at the head of her granddaddy's grave. Her great-grandparents are beside her and her great-great-grandparents are also in the vicinity.

MELANIE'S GRAVE AND MOUNMENT

Perhaps the coup de grâce is "Melanie's Awakening," a bronze dancing figure suspended and reaching heavenward. The concept formed in my mind in the fall of 1991. We located an artist who studied photographs, writings, and video clips of Melanie for two years before he began to mold the wax into its form, the art of lost-wax casting.

MELANIE'S AWAKENING
Melanie Delores Gulledge July 28, 1973 - August 29, 1990

83

MELANIE'S AWAKENING

Presented to Columbia College* by
Van S. and Delores D. Gulledge
In loving memory of their daughter
Melanie Delores Gulledge
July 28, 1973 – August 29, 1990

"I'm dancing and I'm free"

Bronze Sculpture
Artist: Mark Hopkins

*Columbia College, Columbia, South Carolina
A private liberal arts women's college affiliated with
United Methodist Church   www.columbiasc.edu/

Rebirthing a place for Melanie in ongoing family events was a potential challenge. A parent's nightmare is to have their dead child forgotten and feel a sense that the child's life was meaningless. My family has been sensitive in this area in many ways. They call Melanie's name and make references to her in conversation. When my son and daughter-in-love were married, a single long-stem Sonja rose was placed on a chair to hold her space. My daughter-in-law's thoughtfulness in selection of the peach colored rose was a link to the bank of roses that covered Melanie's casket.

My nephew, Melanie's friend and classmate as well as her cousin, hugged me on his wedding day as he said, "Aunt Dee, I miss Melanie being here." Recently, another nephew honored Melanie and other deceased family members at his wedding with a designated flower arrangement.

That same springtime, my niece, who is two years younger than Melanie, was also planning a large church wedding. One morning, I commented to my husband that I had not sensed an awareness of Melanie's presence for a long time. I wondered if she might be on a sacred mission. I received a letter in the mail that same day from my niece telling me about the many times she and Melanie sat on the

85

floor as little girls planning their respective weddings. She said the concept of planning her wedding without Melanie's support was overwhelming for her until one day as she was making some wedding-related choices she sensed an awareness of Melanie. Throughout the remainder of the planning it seemed to her that Melanie was helping. She even reserved a space for Melanie in the wedding party with someone standing in. An overcast sky graced the April day. When stopped for a traffic light on the drive to the church, the bride and her mother, my sister, observed a significant opening in the clouds where the sunlight streamed down. My niece exclaimed, "I knew Melanie would be here for me today." My family is a special gift from God; I am thankful for their continuing support and acknowledgment of Melanie. I feel honored to be a member of such a unique family.

A period has not been placed at the end of Melanie's life. In my value and belief system she is an eternal being. I will continue to honor her space.

Your Turn

What intentional action are you prompted to take to re-birth a place for your loved one?

Write, draw, or doodle your thoughts here.

THE INTENTIONAL ACTION
OF
REINVENTING MYSELF

A HEART CRY

Come into my world
Please won't you come in—
Come in and share the hurt and pain
the sorrow and suffering.

Will you not walk with me?
Walk with me through the cold dark shadows
Will you not hold my hand
through the valley called grief?

Will you not share your strength
and offer your compassion
That is what God put us here for
said Melanie in her lively lilting voice.

"God put us here
to be unselfish
to share our lives
with each other."

So now, I ask you---
Will you risk it?
Will you come into my painful, empty world?
Will you help me heal?

Dee G.
10-18-98

In the aftermath of Melanie's death, I faced painful realities about myself. My identity had to be redefined. My sense of self was lost. My identity was lost. My son was an adult in his college career. My husband had his work. I felt that I had nothing. Even though I was still a wife and a mother, I had lost all sense of identity. I stood alone in the wreckage wondering if there was anything of me to salvage. I had to reclaim and reframe my own life. In the journey that ensued I had to ask how might I take all these facets – wife, mother, daughter, son, husband and the subordination of my identity to be sure the family had everything it needed – and make something out of it all? "I know with a woman's way of knowing that, at least in our contemporary Western world, child death is almost unbearable for a mother."[46]

My grief has changed me. I am not the same person I was before my daughter's diagnosis. I will never be that person again. Parts of me died when my daughter died. Those parts cannot be resurrected – I've tried. I will never get back to my old self. "In grieving we must relearn our very selves, including our characters, histories and roles, and identities that we find in them. We must also relearn our self-confidence and self-esteem."[47]   I wondered, Who am I? Where is my place in the world? What am I to do now? How might I reshape the future in a meaningful way to include Melanie, but to live without her physical presence?

I had to reconsider my life in all of its roles and ponder the question, "Now where is my focus?" Because of that transition, making the choice to channel all the grief and all the decisions into an effort to refocus and reconstruct my life, I now am living my life in terms of what I have learned and experienced. I am who I am, standing, as St. Paul said, "By the grace of God, I am who I am" (ICorinthians 15:10). I am a whole human being ready to plow my life into a role I feel I am uniquely qualified for. Enriched by others, I am whole wherever I am. I cannot crawl back into previous roles. All of what I was has been taken to the potter's wheel to construct all that I am now (Jeremiah 18:2-4).

Because of who I am, it was necessary for me to withdraw into solitude. I am basically a self-reliant individual. It was necessary for me to be alone, even though the solitude increased my feeling of abandonment. Left with the wreckage of a former life, in a sense I was a learner in the

School of Suffering, where I learned the language of grief. I also began to discover the grace of grief. I would not be doing what I do now if the experience had been different. McAdams and others argue, "One's conception of one's identity is largely based on making a coherent story of one's past experiences, present situation, and future goals."[48]

What now is my job? Am I still a mother? Do I still have a daughter? Yes, I know I have a son, and yes, I know I have a husband, but what do I have left to give them? The questions still came, sometimes with their own answers. How can I possibly face tomorrow? "Because He lives, I can face tomorrow," says the old Baptist hymn. We do not grieve as if there is no hope (I Thessalonians 4:13). My spiritual tradition teaches there is life after death and I believe I will see my daughter again. She may be in a different form, perhaps, a different shape; nonetheless, my daughter. But that is in the future, another day, another time. I am now living in the pain of the present. How shall I pass the days? How shall I weigh the moments? How do I mark time? How do I fill the silence? After the death of a child who has been the main focus of a mother's life she may question her identity, as I did, by asking, "Who am I? Am I still that person?

92

What am I going to do now?" We mothers feel lost and lonely.

In my own search for peace I was reminded of the prayer of St. Francis of Assisi, *Make Me an Instrument of Your Peace.*

Lord, make me an instrument of Your peace.
Where there is hatred, let me sow love;
Where there is injury, pardon;
Where there is doubt, faith;
Where there is despair, hope;
Where there is darkness, light;
Where there is sadness, joy.
O, Divine Master,
Grant that I may not so much seek to be
consoled as to console;
To be understood as to understand;
To be loved as to love.
For it is in giving that we receive;
It is in pardoning that we are pardoned;
It is in dying that we are born again to
eternal life.

An inner awakening prompted me to reach out to others in their need. Setting aside a self-centered focus, over time I realized I was giving to

93

others the things I felt I so desperately needed. And, indeed, as consolation was offered to others then I, too, was consoled; as I took time to understand others, I, too, felt more understood; as I allowed my heart to be enlarged and opened to genuinely loving others, then I, too, felt loved. It was in the giving of myself that I received; it was in pardoning and in reestablishing relationships that I was pardoned; and it was in dying to my perception of self that I was born into a new life.

As we search for meaning, "we venture forth on new...life courses. We restructure and reinterpret aspects of our life narratives and the self-understandings based in them. And we re-evaluate and often modify our understandings of our place in the larger scheme of things."[49] This reaction was vividly illustrated when I went to the home of a deceased friend. The family was distraught and shocked by this sudden unexpected death. Yesterday she was healthy, today she was dead. The young adult son sobbed in my embrace as we both sought comfort. Placing my outstretched hand on his heaving abdomen, I thought, this is the beginning of his "griefsong." Being with someone else in grief is really hard; it drains emotions.

One researcher describes the process of offering empathy as "Entering the perceptual world of the other, becoming thoroughly at home in it."[50] Another refers to this process as "companioning," joining the grief journey of another, inviting the bereaved to interpret their unique grief experience.

The natural inclination was to preserve and exalt my daughter's memory, to live my life through her. What freedom could I have? What choices could I make? Captivity was not what I wanted. I was caught in the prison of grief. "...Some people consider their experience with trauma or loss to be the turning point in their lives, a watershed after which their sense of identity or purpose was transformed."[51] Many regard a struggle with loss as a change agent in life, bringing about positive growth. It was for me.

In the context of isolation, I was reminded of my own prayer after Melanie's death. Standing in the bathroom, looking into the mirror as the Associate Pastor stood at the foot of my stairs inquiring, "Dee, can you come down now? There are people here who want to see you, some have driven a long distance to come and their time to be here is very limited." One huge racking silent sob passed like a wave through my body as I inhaled sharply and exhaled slowly, praying, "O, Lord, you know I would rather stay here in solitude, clutching my daughter's memory to myself. Instead I am being called to emerge from my private thoughts in the grief world into public acknowledgment and acceptance of sympathy from others. O, Lord, help me please to allow these people to love me." Realizing my role and responsibility I emerged. On the walk down the stairs God transformed my inner being from a rejecting isolating attitude to an accepting embracing one. It cycled forth and back, but this may have been the intentional beginning of making private public.

"Religious, philosophical, and folk traditions have for thousands of years recognized the possibility that the struggle with major losses in life can be the source of enhanced meaning in life and the impetus for positive change. In some traditional religious accounts—for example, the story of Job in the Christian Old Testament—suffering is paradoxically a result of special favor in the eye of God. In some Islamic traditions, suffering is viewed as instrumental for the purposes of God.

The suffering of Jesus on the cross is interpreted in Christian tradition as the means by which believers are spared the eternal punishment and suffering they justly deserve."[52]

Creativity is easy when life is easy. I could decorate my home, dress my family, plant and arrange flowers, write an "Activities Guide for Parents" for gifted and talented students, and fully participate in the development of a needed program for gifted students. When my life crashed, creativity ceased to be simple. Arranging flowers in a decorative bowl is one thing. A new creation from shattered fragments demands a totally different determined creative response.

I had to take the smashed fragments of my comfortable life and decide what to do with them.

My feelings, too painful to verbalize, were sometimes expressed in writing. I needed time to think and sort through the parts and pieces. I walked and thought and wept and came home to write, sometimes spending hours getting a few sentences on paper. It was as if time stood still. I did not want to miss anything. "Repeatedly confronting the traumatic life event might allow the individual to habituate to it and reduce the stress aroused by the memory."[53]

For years, I had tried to write the story everyone kept asking for, but to no avail. I could only write bits and pieces, capturing snatches of intense emotion in journals, random sheets of paper. Ironically, I always needed paper with lines. I now wonder if in the midst of such mental, emotional, relational and spiritual confusion the lines represented some degree of order and perhaps control. However, I could not write in a single journal dedicated specifically to grief thoughts. The pain was so intense that sometimes once recorded, I was unable to touch the journal, the notebook or the loose pieces of paper or the scraps of napkin or other things that contained the scribbles of emotion. So, I designated a tote bag to contain the outpouring of pain. When the bulging bag would no longer hold another scrap I dubbed a box a continuing container. Hours, days, weeks, months and years of writings and tape recordings expressing internal pain, thoughts and feelings were squirreled away in my secret box.

Scribbling notes and writing thoughts were a way of externalizing painful emotions without fear of judgment. No one suggested writing to me as a means of expressing grief; it came spontaneously after the death of my daughter. I remembered hearing her say, "I'm on a roll, let me finish this please." Feeling alone and isolated, I found writing was a way of giving voice to strong emotions. Writing prose or poetry allows all emotions to spill out, the good, the bad, and the ugly, uninhibited. Writing used as an emotional expression or for healing is about the details of everyday life. It may be about disbelief, anger, frustration, emptiness, loneliness or any other grief related issue. For several years I included "Melanie, too" in parentheses underneath our name when cards were signed. At birthdays and holidays, I often selected cards for my husband and son and sometimes for myself that expressed sentiments our daughter might choose.

Researching and reflecting on the contents of packed away journals, notebooks and scraps of paper uncovered the layering of my life, the crossroads, pathways and the miles traveled on my grief journey. When the conscious mind was unable to string words together for verbal expression, the unconscious could record lived experience in writing. It requires enormous courage to expose script written with such deep honest intensity. Current and future generations need to understand the profound depth, intensity and longevity of pain over the death of a child. I have chosen to unlock the pages of my secret writings in an effort to teach, inspire and help others. "Writing is a powerful vehicle for self-discovery, understanding, and healing." It can help us understand the past, see the present more clearly, and offer clues for the future. Internal transformation may take place at any point along the way.[54]

My first creative effort resulted in a guide for surviving grief. Almost faster than my hand could write, words and tears poured out of me onto the paper. To demonstrate the concept and to indicate the release of pent up emotions, the guide is reprinted here.

GRIEF SURVIVAL GUIDE:
WHEN YOU LOSE SOMEONE YOU LOVE

By Delores Dalrymple Gulledge

Dedicated to the memory of my daughter
Melanie
July 28, 1973 - August 29, 1990
She taught me how to live with a grief too deep for tears.

At times I must be silent and stoic to protect myself. At other times I need someone who will listen, helping me accept my limits as I explore the secret places of my heart.

Dear God, Help me please:

Just for today—the pain is so intense, the hurt so deep, the emptiness so real. How is it possible to go on? Help me focus on this minute, this hour, this day only, and leave the tomorrows in your care. Today Lord, just for today I'll think on You as I remember this message from an old song "One day at a time, sweet Jesus, one day at a time."

Just for today—I'm hurting so badly I'm not sure I can bear up under the stress of pain. I don't really want anyone to know how much I hurt. In fact I don't even know how to form the words to express the pain. I don't even know how to tell God how much I hurt. But just today I'll try. I'll sit before Him in silence. My tears, my heart, the groans from my innermost being will be my tools of communication.

Just for today—I refuse to drown in the wave of grief that has engulfed me. I will deliberately call out for help. I will telephone a friend. If that friend is not available I will call another and another if I must to find someone who is available...Someone who will listen to my silence and not be offended by my tears.

Just for today—I need my friends so much right now. I need someone to understand my pain, but I know they can't. I need someone who will not pity me, but love me. I need someone to share their strength with me. I need their warmth. I need their caring presence. I need the comfort of a hug. I need someone who will not be afraid of my tears or my angry outburst of emotion. I am weak, but they are strong. I need to allow someone to carry me, just for today.

Just for today—I will understand that my friends love me and care for me. I will understand that they have jobs and families and responsibilities that claim their attention. I will understand that just because I don't hear from them doesn't mean they don't care for me. Just for today I'll write down my thoughts, my feelings, even my silence.

Just for today—I will not isolate myself in my world of hurt and pain. I will go for a walk. I will notice the trees reaching upward, the pansies braving the chill with their bright faces turned heavenward. I will notice the squirrels scampering and the birds singing. I, too will turn my face upward expressing gratitude for the creation of nature, for my breath, for my life, and for the butterflies.

Just for today—I will try to understand that my friends do not know what I need. Some of them want to cheer me up and make me laugh. They don't understand the depth of my sadness and loss and my fear that I'll never feel like laughing again. My life has changed. My experiences separate me from them. I cannot go back to the way it was. They cannot step into my world and really know what it is like. Just for today I will accept that our lives are different.

Just for today—I will give myself permission to weep and yes, to scream if I feel like it. Permission to embrace the grief and feel the pain. Permission to curl into a fetal position and collapse on the floor in an attempt to protect myself from the suffering. I will realize there is no protection, no amount of pretending will banish the hurt. I give myself permission to believe that life will be better tomorrow.

Just for today—I long to know someone cares, but I am too embarrassed to let them know how much I still hurt. But today I will say to someone, "I need you to listen. I need you to share a memory of my dear one with me."

Just for today—I'll admit how hard grief work is. I'll allow myself some extra rest. My body is exhausted from the emotional struggle. Today I'll put the struggle aside and succumb to sweet and peaceful sleep.

Just for today—Help me to remember to thank those dear ones who have helped me learn to live with the grief. Most of all please help me remember to give thanks to God for never forsaking me.

104

Just for today—Help me find meaning in the fire that burns in my soul. Help me understand how my suffering, my pain, my hurt, my experiences can help me grow. Help me sort through the feelings. Help me know how to use my experiences to benefit others.

Just for today—I'll take all my pain, all my hurt, all my suffering to Jesus. I'll wrap it in a bundle and I'll sacrifice it all. I'll place my load on the altar at the foot of the cross. By giving it to Jesus, I will believe He will take my offering and make something beautiful.

Just for today—Lord, help me focus on someone else. Help me to offer a smile or a kind word to someone else. Help me be sensitive to the hurts and needs of another—to listen—to care—for someone else.

Additional copies of this guide are available for a nominal fee. Contact Delores Gulledge at: drdee@artsasmedicine.com

Clutching this written outpouring of feelings to myself was one thing, but releasing it for others to read was exposing the private inner suffering and pain to the outer world. In searching myself thoroughly to discover the depth of my desire and commitment to reach out to others, I was reminded of the biblical story of the sisters, Mary and Martha (Luke 10:38-42). I wondered if releasing the *Grief Survival Guide* was my costly fragrance.

For Mary of Bethany, breaking the alabaster box containing the precious costly fragrance and allowing it to flow freely over the feet of Jesus was an extravagant act of devotion. Misunderstood by many, perhaps not even understanding herself, Mary was somehow mysteriously drawn to her friend, Jesus. Her focus so intense, her devotion so deep, she risked alienating family and friends when she deliberately placed herself before His feet.

Earlier, her sister, Martha, had complained that Mary had abandoned her in the kitchen as food preparation was in progress. Blessed with three sisters myself, I can easily understand the strong feelings that might erupt if four of us sisters were working together preparing for dinner guests when suddenly one of us escapes to sit in on the conversation with company. Perhaps not even contributing to the conversation, but rather sitting

106

near, gazing into the face, mesmerized not only by the words of truth flowing from His mouth, but also by His countenance and authority. I like to believe that Mary was treating every word as a treasure, tucking each thought away in her heart.

Perhaps Mary had a contemplative nature. Could it be that as she quietly went about her tasks over the next days and weeks, she would pull forth first one treasure and then another from her heart, turning it over and over in her mind? Inside her head, she could hear the voice of Jesus teaching. Perhaps as the authority and truth of the words moved from her head into her heart, the adoring love and devotion for the Master grew into an unexplainable pristine intimacy.

Could it be possible that she heard Jesus say, "Anyone who comes to me but refuses to let go of father, mother, spouse, children, brothers, sisters – yes, even one's own self! – can't be my disciple" (Luke 14:26)? Simply put, if you are not willing to take what is dearest to you, whether plans or people, and hold it in an open hand, you can't be my disciple.

Could it be Mary counted the cost? Perhaps the special box with its fragrant ointment was her most prized personal possession. I wondered if it symbolized what she held dearest to her heart.

As I identified with Mary, I also wondered if Jesus is filled with joy when I live with abandon for

Him, when I release my hold on this or that image of myself. When I am willing to admit my brokenness, releasing its hold on me? When I am willing to spill out the suffering of my pain and hurt over the grief of my daughter to help someone else? Can I unbind her and let her go, offering to Jesus the costly fragrance of my intense and private pain? In the innermost sanctuary of my heart, I perceived Jesus asking, "Dee, will you do it for me?"

It is one thing to open a bottle of costly perfume and share it around in measured amounts one drop at a time. It is entirely another to crush the decorative container, allowing the fragrance to spill out completely at will, never to be recovered and confined again.

In the years since Melanie's death, from time to time I had shared experiences of God's provision and His sustaining grace throughout her sickness and death. God supervised the invitations, creating a time and a place for measured amounts of pain to be released – a drop of fragrance here and a drop there. But never before had I felt the freedom to crush the protective covering of privacy, sharing with openness and honesty the raw pain of my grief over the death of my daughter. This expressed my feelings as I released the *Grief Survival Guide*.

As a symbol of this "breaking open," I crushed a bottle of perfume called "No Regrets" and buried the gold top near another child's grave in the autumn of 1997.

Through such actions, I came to see that faith involves openness to profound change. Faith does not mean denying an unpleasant reality in order to hang on to a preconceived idea. Faith demands confronting clear truth with a profound conviction that God is enough. And His ways, which are far beyond our understanding, can effect a transformation beyond comprehension. Nothing is beyond the transforming power of the Almighty God (Luke 1:37).

Posttraumatic growth refers to positive change that results from the struggle with a major loss or trauma. Growth may be described as a "changed sense of self, changed relationships, and changed philosophy of life."[55] Cognitive coping strategies seemed to help many mothers "transform their experience from one of pain to one of growth and meaning."[56]

Cultural foundations and expectations about grieving, mourning, and/or bereavement may influence methods of grief expression in the action of reinventing oneself. The bereaved may feel unable to articulate the loss in all its complexity in traditional verbal methods. One or more components of expressive art may be offered as a means of expression. Sometimes an individual may be able to write when they cannot verbalize; or they may be able to visually express the pain; or another option may be tactile with textures and shapes revealing inner feelings; or perhaps music may stir memories and images; movement is yet another means for externalizing the internal pain of grief.

No one can predict which of the expressive arts might offer release for a bereaved individual. Some creative options may be rejected, and several may be experimented with, before a bereaved individual discovers an art as the channel for expressing grief. Traditional facilitation of the grief experience usually means engaging the bereaved in verbal interaction. Perhaps symbolizing the grief experience in one or more of the creative arts might open someone for the grief to emerge as a means of expression and release.

In my experience with a sense of loss of confidence, competence and power, I explored new ways of interaction and socialization. After an interlude of several years with walking being my only physical outlet, I tentatively entered the study of martial arts with mounting self-doubt about my ability to learn the simplest techniques. Initially, learning karate uniform etiquette with adjusting and tying the belt seemed like an enormous task. With a grief-laden heart and prevailing sadness I sought some relief in karate. It was an emotional and mental struggle just to get out of the house and get to class. "One mother reported, 'I wanted to scream, but was unable to utter a sound for fear of shattering some delicate thread within, which was holding me together.'"[57] Encouraged by my husband and a young female college student, I plodded along until an inner motivation began to develop. Karate was indeed outside the perception of my limitations. Many bereaved adults interviewed by researchers "said they had developed new skills, done things they had never done before, were thankful that they no longer had to rely so much on other people, felt more mature, and were now better able to face a crisis if one emerged."[58]

I also entered into a profound and constantly deepening appreciation of the extraordinary beauty of nature in all of its details: the colorful butterfly lighting delicately on an exquisite flower, the shape of a cloud that resembled the dancing form of my slender and graceful daughter, the sweet budding of a red rose in my backyard, the view of mountains from the porch of a house, and the always comforting presence of the ocean in all its ebbing and surging tides on a windswept beach. Sensory experiences influenced my spiritual, emotional and mental state and my creative expression. I began to develop a heightened and focused relationship between myself and elements of nature.

Some researchers have explored the use of photographs with bereaved parents. When parents shared photographs, they moved from dwelling on the death of the child to remembering stories about the child's life. Photographs provided an opportunity to reflect and remember events, treasured experiences, and/or the everyday antics of the dead child. "This may facilitate conversations and reminiscences about the living relationship and enable introduction of the deceased child to people who did not know him or her." Researchers point out that in interviews with bereaved parents, they were frequently introduced to the dead child through photographs.[59] "There are those who loved Melanie in life and there will be others who will love her in death."[60]

Engaging in photography as a visual art opened avenues for remembering and sharing

Melanie's life. Her death is a fact that I cannot change. Photographs are a reminder of shared activities and events with family and friends. Researching my databank of photographs was a bittersweet experience of memories mingled with the realization they would have to last my lifetime. An additional, current and ongoing photographic record of her physical life was no longer possible. I discovered one way of preserving memories is "Scrapping your grief," a painful but healing process of gathering and reframing photographs. The process of reframing photographs became an intentional effort of redefining and reframing my life while remembering Melanie.

After Melanie's death, nature seemed to call me in a new way. Focusing on intricate aspects of flowers, birds, butterflies and landscapes seemed to be therapeutic, instilling a sense of peaceful calm. Wilderness therapy in the African savannah and bush country provided photographic opportunities for capturing emotional expression. An expanded awareness of cycles of life and death in nature seemed to contribute to acceptance of the reality of death that over time transitioned to reconciliation. Setting aside the controlling critical aspect of perfectionism, capturing visual images on photographic film fed my creative spirit. Perception of creative images is influenced by one's attitude. The power of photographs may help bereaved parents move forward from a feeling of distress to a sense of de-stress. Sharing photographs seems to contribute to diffusing bereavement-related stress. For others, photographs and reminder objects may be a source of pain and they may be put away immediately. I have been a witness to the quick disposal of reminder items. If this is a short-term solution it may aid temporary coping; however, "when the bereaved quickly gets rid of all the things associated with the deceased … it could lead to a complicated grief reaction."[61] Parents who are far along in their grief begin to find a new balance in life. Letting go of the identity with the child's pain, they no longer continually reach for a positive bond with the dead child. Shifting the identity with pain to identity with the love that was in the living child contributes to the new life balance. Developing bonds related to the life of the child, rather than the death of the child, sometimes contributes to healing.

For me, in the struggle to fill the emptiness and find a new way to live my life, I sometimes felt I was more Melanie than myself. Occasionally, people would comment that they felt as if they were seeing Melanie rather than me. A new acquaintance inquired, "Are you a dancer? You moved with such gracefulness I just knew you must be a dancer yourself." I wondered if the graceful fluid movements were her expression. All too often, the inner me still saw myself as an awkward, klutzy adolescent who found it easier to walk into tables rather than sidestep them, when in actuality it seems my movements appeared to express a sense of fluidity and grace.

Can it be that my newfound ability to write is really Melanie's thoughts and feelings seeking expression through me? Can it be that my sense of celebration is her expression of "loving a party?" I did not mimic her life, but have taken on some of her interests as my own. Could it be my sense of style and color is the expression of her desire to model and walk the runway? Could it be that when I wear Melanie's earth tone colors of beige, brown, champagne, olive green, peach, orange and chartreuse that I somehow become her, even down to skin tone? Reflecting, I remember at times saying, "I feel like Melanie in this outfit." However, I never felt there were separate personalities in the same body, but a mixing, blending and folding aspects of her life into mine that over time created or invented something new. This new connection is not selfish assimilation, but a means of honoring and extending Melanie's existence. Parental identification with a deceased child is not unexpected and is acceptable in appropriate amounts. However, if identification with the deceased child is so complete the parent loses a sense of personal identity, the process has become unhealthy.

It would be unhealthy to keep her alive by trying to live out her life, but the conscious and/or unconscious blending has contributed to the recreation or reinvention of myself. Could it possibly be that her love for others and desire to serve, giving freely and tirelessly, unselfishly and unconditionally, is her greatest gift of all to me? Could it be that through her gift, the gift of self to my self, that the qualities, sensitiveness, and attributes that made her so uniquely Melanie have enmeshed into the psyche of me, her mother; that the two have reconciled and a true oneness has been achieved?

Integrating aspects of Melanie into my life has sparked a desire to try new things, to create, to discover, and to make caring investments. This has been one way of retaining a lasting connection with my daughter. "The end of grief is not a severing of the bond with the dead child, but an integration of the child into the parent's life in a different way than when the child was alive."[62]

A paradox of the grief experience is that while it may be the worst experience of a lifetime, it may also result in positive outcomes. Grief researchers have recently begun to explore the positive outcomes from bereavement. They do not, yet, know the breadth of the relationship between bereavement and positive outcome. This may be an area for future research. "The positive aspects of bereavement do not contradict or diminish the painful and frequently nightmarish effects of death; rather, they slowly and unexpectedly emerge as the dawn of healing replaces the lonely darkness of grief."[63] Further, Frantz reports that one indication of positive outcome from a painful and/or traumatic experience is the ability to complete simple daily tasks required for living. Engaging in meaningful activities is also an indication of positive outcome.

Current bereavement literature indicates that the bereavement period is filled with choices. The choices an individual makes influence the outcome of the grief experience after an undesirable event. Some bereaved individuals who have searched for meaning and tried to sort out the good from the loss have reported benefits of character growth that changed them for the better. They reported gaining a different perspective of what is important in life.

Another benefit is stronger relationships, gained by appreciating the value of family and friends.

In a study where parents indicated their grief was resolved (to the extent it will be), they concluded, "You don't get over your grief, you learn to live with it in a different way as it changes over time." Transitioning the bond with the deceased child may require extended effort and energy over a long time. "Dead children are often melded into the parent's better self in a way that makes the children seem like teachers of life's important lessons."[64]

My mind continued to question and sometimes to answer. With my grief reconciled as much as it can be at this time, what is my job, my mission in life now? To say the things often left unsaid, to work toward harmony within others and myself? To teach others to value every minute of every day? To remind individuals that each breath is a gift in and of itself? Is that what I'm here for? I have discovered over time that my mission is not self-sabotage, but enhancement of self-worth. Not to run from God shaking my fist, but to find security and safety in the arms of God. To value myself enough to venture out into unexplored territory. It is my job to pioneer, to prepare myself to help others understand the long lonely journey through grief from a child's death and other losses. Just to help others know they are not alone, and that someone relates to the pain and suffering of giving up a child to death, is a valuable gift. "Part of the resolution of grief is making the child's death and the experience of it count for something. One of the ways parents' lives can count, and the child be real, is to help others."[65]

The action of reinventing myself included, over time, embracing Melanie's love for creative activities, taking risks, seeing familiar things from a new perspective and trying new things. Creative expression may become an integral part of the process in the search for meaning in loss. Initially, the desire to do something was an effort to assuage the pain. The will to act was weak, but three different dreams shared a common theme, with me sinking, spiraling downward. Perhaps the fear of losing myself in the black hole of grief, combined with the drive to make meaning from a seemingly senseless loss, propelled me into action. Together, my husband and I made a conscious decision that we did not want the suffering and pain of loss wasted. Symbolically, we offered the complete

119

experience to God asking that it be used to help others.

A friend gave me a cassette tape saying she thought of me when she heard the melody. That very day while my husband and I were on a road trip, we listened to the comforting soothing sounds of the music. The sound seemed to be ethereal, opening grief-laden spaces within us. We drove for hours in silence as the tape repeated itself continuously. The music seemed to lift us, to carry us, but yet to also comfort and hold us in our pain. The tape became a constant companion for every mile we traveled until one day, more than a year later, it seemed to disappear. Searching the house, the car, the suitcases, the tote bags, everywhere time and again the tape could not be located. Bewildered, but not defeated, I continued the futile search in music stores by describing the angels on the cover. I did not know the name of the music or the artist. I only knew it soothed our souls. Unable to duplicate or adequately describe the melody, the cassette has never been replaced. It did the work of teaching me the power of music for solace. "Music does not make people unhappy…it lifts the lid off emotions which are already there, hidden below the surface."[66]

Academically, I was introduced to theory and practice of the power of sound as healing. This opened avenues for mourning previously unknown to me. Vibration, toning, harmonics and the power of using the voice as a healing instrument relaxed and energized at the same time. Engaging music as medicine was therapeutic and transforming, with sounds reaching untouched areas of grief pain. Jonathan Goldman's work with *Healing Sounds* focuses on harmonics that create vibrational change. This use of sound to explore the inner landscape, creating change, was known and used by the ancients, but lost to modern society until its recent revival in the 1980's. Experiencing sound, without a focus on understanding it, seems to transcend everyday thoughts. Vibrations without melody seem to awaken the body and mind to another level of awareness.

Experienced in a new way, music opened my awareness and stimulated my mind. It seemed as if this not only invited me, but also gave me permission to risk more grief expression in creative arts activities.

The soft glow of candles and the soothing voice of the instructor created a calm atmosphere for my initial adventure with modeling clay. Poised, but hesitatingly, my extended hands met the cool, smooth, gray clay, producing a profound unforgettable moment for me. Touching the clay reminded me of touching my daughter's face after her death. Stunned and immobilized, I sat in silence reflecting and remembering the feel of Melanie's skin under my fingertips. Slowly returning to the present, I followed the instructor's directions. During the processing of the workshop, I gave voice to my intense tactile encounter. Awareness of the sensory experience remains in my memory. An experience of the senses may communicate at a level deeper than words.

Expressive arts had an important role in facilitating my grief journey. Experiencing the arts culminated in a tangible example of my reinvention. Movement, music, visual art, tactile art, writing and verbal expression summarized my process of transformation into the invention of "Griefsong." "Griefsong" externalizes the affective and represents a visual expression of the action of healing that transformed my narrative.

My life has been refined and redefined. I have new dreams and desires. The "me" in transition wanted to say, "Give me a chance, you might like me."

Seemingly, the outside format of my life did not change. I still get up every Sunday morning and go to church at Riverland Hills Baptist Church; however, my activities, focus and participation are completely changed. I did not turn away from family or faith. However, my relationship with both is dramatically different. Even now I will keep on going to the same church unless I sense that God sends me in another direction.

Your Turn

What intentional action are you prompted to take to reinvent yourself?

Write, draw, or doodle your thoughts here.

THE INTENTIONAL ACTION
OF
RE-CREATING THE STORY
THROUGH "GRIEFSONG"

At the inception of this experience, the concept of presenting a movement-oriented piece for others to witness was beyond my grasp. I walked into my daughter's world, a world of hardwood floors, mirrors, and a barre stabilized against the wall. The intimidation factor of the mirrors alone was enough to send me scurrying. But, I had made a commitment for a compensatory project. It was something I needed to complete. There I was, looking at myself, staring back at myself, perhaps seeing for the first time the evident ravages of grief.

In the process of re-creating the story, weeks of dialogue with a movement mentor were required for the verbal externalization of the grief narrative. My grief experience brought back the intensity of pain as if it was brand new. Self-regulating, I distanced myself from this project from time to time. Research indicates that rest does not produce insights; it provides a state of relaxation. It is the relaxation state that allows creativity to be released. All the while, the grief experience was incubating just below the conscious level. There was a strong desire to visit my daughter's gravesite. The two-hour drive was filled with a mixture of tears and smiles as memories mingled. Mourning, speaking aloud, sitting in silence, pulling up stray blades of grass, rearranging the seashells one more time and arranging new flowers on her grave seemed to fill me with a sense of peace. The return miles were consumed with thoughts of what might have been.

Translating words, emotions, and experiences into movement was an arduous process for me. It was new and felt very uncomfortable. Experimenting with hand and body gestures with increased awareness of body alignment, muscle control and balance added a new dimension to bereavement. It was a physically exhausting, but somehow exhilarating experience. The expenditure of emotional energy from the action of telling the story required time for emotional recovery. Public and private layers of an experience unfold as movement accompanies a story. The story may reveal emotional layers of feelings associated with the struggle with loss. The story creates images. Through movement, images are presented to one's social environment.

Using karate as my method and form of movement expression triggered an epiphany: even though I was engaged in fighting mode, I could choose the enemy and the outcome. The action of participating in karate disorganized the distress in my muscles by reorganizing rigid tense muscles with release, contraction and breathing techniques. This developed an awareness of muscle groups and the ability to contract and release muscle intensity at will. My body contained so much that needed to be unlocked. Relearning a portion of my body's capacity contributed to reforming the physical appearance and creating a new self-image. Collaboratively, selected karate kata movements were analyzed to build this specific piece.

Alone in the studio, on my birthday, sensing the presence of my daughter was a powerful wonderful gift. Experiencing the nearness of her in this space so familiar to her was overwhelming. It felt as if the studio was filled with light and fragrance and graceful lilting lifting movement. The hard karate moves gained new definition with gracefulness. Her nearness seemed to unlock inhibitions, inviting me to dance with her. With no one to judge, releasing the rigidity of my form, I moved freely and gracefully with fluidity that was a new experience for me. This altered state of consciousness provided a "powerfully transformative sense of oneness."[67] Physically, I discovered the meaning of turning mourning into dancing. Movement invention is not defined by style, form or technique. It provides an opportunity to move, simply meeting the need to move. Even now, drawing the experience from the treasure chest of memories is deeply moving.

Characteristic of my husband, he entered the dance making process with a playful and teasing – almost flippant – attitude. I found this somewhat irritating, until I reminded myself that he was establishing his place. I also remembered I had been in the studio for weeks. He was exploring and wondering what would be asked of him. Listening, half-heartedly at first, and then carefully, he became a willing participant. In this piece, I wanted to allude to some gender differences and incongruence between husband and wife in grief expression. I wanted to acknowledge the possibility of conflict as parents seek to regain stability. Also, I wanted to propose that intentional commitment might be the glue to keep a marriage intact for bereaved parents.

Variety and a sense of professionalism were added to the project through the introduction of the senior student dance major, who was the recipient of Melanie's scholarship. Having her portray the spirit of Melanie, touching, holding, lifting, transporting Melanie's mementoes from one corner to another, while wearing a garment belonging to me over her dancing clothes, tweaked my heart. Realizing the dancer was a representation, not the reality, of my daughter, focused my attention toward coaching her. Sharing the significance of locked boxes, photographs, teddy bears and garments gave meaning to movements. Replicating some of my hard intensely controlled movement with light, graceful delicate motion created a noticeable contrast between our moves. Having her mimic me, encourage me and brush my body with her hands extended my sensory perception of Melanie's presence. Witnessing her freedom of spirit and graceful artful dance with the butterfly ribbons reaffirmed Melanie's life transition and transformation.

129

After several trial and error staging experiments, we settled on four corners that connected principally with straight movement from death to memory, memory to death, memory to home and home to memory. Diagonal movements connected memory to heaven. The tightrope intersected stage middle on a plane half way between death and heaven. An open spiraling freedom layered the structured lines.

Melanie's spirit dancer could never go into the corner of death. She was beyond it. She had transcended the natural life and the natural world, joining the supernatural realm of joy and peace forevermore. Her life was good on earth, but now, it is so much better. She exhibited freedom of movement between the "Memory Corner," the "Home Corner," and the "Heaven Corner." She even skirted the edge of the "Death Corner," once when she came near me, and then again when she claimed her daddy's attention.

Outward physical manifestations of grief were depicted in the tense tight controlled movements of my body. Training physical abilities is one way to "perfect ... mental insight and emotional sensitivity."[68] This contrasted with the defeated, dejected, curled fetal position in an attempt to escape that horrible searing pain. The pain of loneliness, of lostness, of emptiness seemed to be ever present. The pain of losing, of loving and of losing physical attachment was intense. There were feeble attempts to push myself shakily upward, crawling before walking; pushing deliberately forward while wondering if it was really backward. It felt like step, drag and struggle searching for a way out of the fog of confused slow motion. The human body forms a shape that reveals tension when life rhythm is interrupted. The body absorbs "words, thoughts, emotions and muscular gestures" connected with an event.[69]

My husband, laden with the vestiges of his workday, revealed slumped shoulders and a collapsed chest. Posture speaks of heritage, life experiences and psychological states. Approaching him, unloading him, embracing him in a sense shared my energy. "Two are better off than one, because together they can work more effectively. If one of them falls down, the other can help him up" (Ecclesiastes 4:9-10). When my husband was distracted by the clapping hands his posture shifted. Emotional shock triggers a startle reflex that may contribute to feelings of despair and helplessness in prolonged disarrangement. Intentional physical responses may change the arrangement of the body from a defeated image to a confident stance.

Intentionally, I moved into the memories. Going back into the moment when Melanie's spirit dancer watched delightedly, I unwrapped the box cradling the precious porcelain doll she had so lovingly, carefully, secretly made for me. Setting the eyes, painting the delicate strokes of eyebrows, the clarity of it all. Carefully lifting her up, lifting her high, the doll that won the blue ribbon prize at the South Carolina State Fair.

When conceptualized ideas became concrete, the piece was birthed, taking on a life of its own, growing and maturing as music, staging and technical aspects were added. Then I was faced with a decision. Was this work only for my private edification or for public witness? Weighing the consequences, the inner struggle was brief. I seemed to know that the action of releasing the visual expression of my grief narrative for public witness would contribute to my healing and may also have potential for helping others heal.

For me, it required an enormous amount of courage to move beyond my perceived limits. "The discipline of creation is a mix of surrender and initiative."[70]

132

Even now, I know that I created, participated and performed, but sometimes it seems as if I were standing on another plane, watching from afar. Watching someone other than myself moving, soaring, twirling, leaping, graceful as a gazelle, maybe never to be recaptured and repeated. But then, perhaps, it is there in the shadows waiting, just waiting to be called forth to emerge into the everyday, allowing the free spirit to become the ordinary rather than the exception, if only in private.

I found that intentionally engaging in creative action to interpret a personal grief experience into non-verbal language may be a "process [that] moves from what has happened, to what is, to what can be, until it becomes what will be."[71] Shaping something new from experiences of the past and present transforms the narrative for the future. Personal experience with death may cause one to see through new eyes, hear with new ears, feel with deeper sensitivity, and express fully through intentional physical movements.

THE INTENTIONAL ACTION
OF
RELEASING THE STORY
THROUGH "GRIEFSONG"

The videotaped presentation of a live performance of "Griefsong," performed in Cottingham Theatre at Columbia College, opened with a stage set in four different areas. As the curtain opens, the audience sees, in the "Home Corner," a child-sized empty rocking chair draped with dress-up clothes, a reminder of emptiness and a sense of lostness that seems to pervade the atmosphere. Occupying the adult companion chair, Van is searching the Holy Book for comfort and for answers that do not exist in this lifetime. Sitting in semidarkness, he is absorbed by what he is reading, when suddenly there is a scream that pierces the blackness. My scream of terror, of horror at the mere thought of having the life of my daughter taken away. A light appears, revealing a mother dressed in a karate uniform. The intruder is

135

imagined and causes the warrior mother to react. The fight is on. Horrible hurtful blows are made to the most vulnerable parts of the anatomy. They were blows that would cripple a strong man and terrify a weak one. Crumpling, the crippled foe fell to the floor. To ensure the demise of the unwanted shadow foe, I deliberately went to the floor also. Kicking and screaming again and again for full force and power, I pummeled the intruder. The foe is defeated; death is defeated, no more to rear its ugly head.

The "Memory Corner" was filled with symbols that are reminders of Melanie: the doll, music boxes, dancing shoes, bridesmaid nosegay of silk flowers, a large photograph of her dominating the central point, smaller ones of her with others, miniature perfume bottles, Bible, Acteens crown and scepter, jewelry box, boxes and more boxes large and small holding treasures of the heart, hat, awards and plaques and other things. In this corner of memories there was also a dancer. The dancer, representing Melanie's spirit, was near, touching my daughter's things, even opening a music box to hear the tune. I released the need to clutch her things to myself.

So absorbed in my grief, I was completely unaware of the spirit dancer's presence. I dejectedly but consciously returned to my circle of struggle to ward off the questions, doubts and guilt that could have consumed me, resigned to do the work of grief, the hard work of absorbing the loss that I symbolically acknowledged in lifting up, caressing and holding the doll made by Melanie in the "Memory Corner." Meanwhile, the dancer unwound satin ribbons to remove her ballet shoes, signifying the unbinding from earthly life to a higher plane. She then moved freely, easily dancing gracefully to the strains of music. Moving toward the now empty "Home Corner," she fingered and then slipped on mother's nightgown twirling and showing off, playing dress-up as young girls might do. Traversing the stage dancing, even mimicking my controlled hard blocks, punches and stances with graceful charm, she came near, but never entered the "Death Corner." In my belief system there is life after death; she, having moved into another realm, cannot revisit death.

The pain of the separation was evidenced in the continuing fight of the mother through a repetition of moves and surprise tactics. Accustomed to directing my life outward, it became necessary to turn inward to sort out and define myself in the bereavement experience. This was interrupted by my husband's entrance from work, laden with the stress and pain and burden of his own grief. Weary shoulders, drooping body, and silver hair were outward physical manifestations of the internal pain of loss. Moving quickly toward him, I reached for the hug greeting he had grown accustomed to over the years, but was hampered by the load in his arms. There is an order to things: first I helped him unload, before his arms were free to share the embrace. After helping him remove his coat, laying aside the symbols of his workday, my arm encircled his shoulders as he animatedly related the events of his day.

If a father feels he must not show his emotional pain in an effort to be strong for other family members, he may experience a sense of resentment. Socialization and biblical roles tend to cast the father as protector, provider and problem solver. When a child repeatedly is subjected to unsuccessful treatment and/or dies, the father may be devastated by a sense of failure.

"A father may do some very foolish things … in an effort to escape his own grief."[72]

Suddenly, his attention was diverted and I retreated off stage. Awakening his playful nature, the spirit of Melanie laughed, clapped and told secrets with him, all the while glancing quickly over their shoulder to ensure my absence.

Melanie was the trained dancer, but her daddy had natural rhythm that encouraged toe-tapping routines. He took a moment to show his talent, inviting the spirit of Melanie to try it his way.

I, the mother, reentered the stage, walking the floor as a tightrope walker, a journey I walked for years in an effort to adjust to life without Melanie. I wondered if it were possible to place one foot in front of the other. I wondered if it was worth the effort. Teetering and tottering, my movements were carefully controlled, as was my nature, fearing that if I ever let go I would be unable to regain the illusive footing on what was once the foundation of my life. Still uncertain and tentative about exploring new adjustments in my life, I was completely oblivious to the beckoning, cheering, encouraging spirit of Melanie that was so near. Making a last intentional leap, represented by a firm stance, in complete silence deliberately facing the darkness, I bowed, requesting permission to begin. I fought another fight, a very hard fight, realizing that it would likely not be the last, but resigned to never give up. I was released from the downward spiral of depression and despair. I wondered if this represented the same choice my Mother made after my father's death when she posted a paper in her kitchen with these words: "I don't like it. I can't change it. But I *will* learn to live with it." **I released self-destructive thoughts.**

Lilting music, repeated for emphasis, resumed, reiterating Melanie was not of this world. According to the lyrics, she did not come to add anything. She came to just "be." I continued yet another struggle that seemed somewhat different, still controlled but softer and more graceful as the spirit of Melanie brushed my head and back. With greater contemplative naked awareness I sensed the presence of my precious daughter. Wishing it could last forever, my arms stretched upward entreating her to remain near, while at the same time realizing she had returned to her ethereal world represented by the "Heaven Corner." As my struggle was in process near center stage, she was moving diagonally, transitioning special items, her teddy bear and a music box, from the "Memory Corner" to the "Heaven Corner."

The lovely inviting "Heaven Corner" was filled with open airy tulle and chiffon, the type often worn by dancers. The space was strewn with ribbons, lace, rose petals and leaves. An angel statue graced the edge and a large beautiful, filigree gold box claimed the central point. Spirit of

Melanie settled in the heavenly space to watch her parents. Grief is a heart journey with memories tucked away as treasures. Treasures may be locked in the secret places of the heart where no one is allowed to enter; they may be sacrificed to help one grow and transcend the pain; or they may be transferred to an open filigree box to be shared and then returned for another time. **I released my determined tightfisted hold on her.**

After sensing the spirit of Melanie during my final struggle, I noticed my waiting watching husband who, grasping the Bible, had returned to his chair in the "Home Corner." As I bowed to honor the conclusion of the struggle, my husband approached me with outstretched hand, inviting me to once again become fully present to our marriage. Uncertain, my shaking hand reached, retreated, and then reached again. I released the hold on my defenses. Placing my hand in his, allowing him to lead me back into the "Home Corner," I began to untie my tight confining belt to symbolically begin the slow removal of my protective armor. **I released my self-sufficient attitude.**

I accepted my husband's assistance with the removal of my stiffly starched white gi coat. And I allowed him to help me into a softly flowing pink robe with matching feather-laden high heel sandals.

Next, he helped release the tightly wound severely styled hair to discover cascading rainbow ribbons. Proudly, he paraded me in circles to show me off and to celebrate my homecoming.

Embracing and relaxing body tension before turning outward to face the "Heaven Corner," we watched the ethereal spirit of Melanie draw ribboned butterflies from the open filigree box before she pirouetted and freely gracefully danced encircled by a rainbow of ribbons calling out, *"Mom, look Mom. I'm dancing and I'm free."*

The joyful spirit rejuvenated and transformed me. As darkness settled, a yellow fluttering butterfly appeared as the last strains of music faded.

THE INTENTIONAL ACTION
OF
EXPRESSING DEEP PERSONAL
FEELINGS THROUGH "GRIEFSONG"

I released my feelings of anger in the battle with death. I lay shocked, spent and weary, curled in a fetal position protecting all that is dear, all that is holy, lingering to feel the pain of the event. Wondering, "How, how on earth shall I come out of this alive? How can I live now that my daughter has died?"

With great effort and pain, I push myself, push my body to the limit, forcing the knees to bear my weight, barely able to move, slowly lifting my head to a light that was drawing me. As I dragged myself, I remembered Jacob's struggle (Genesis 32:24-25) and wondered if my foot was lame. Was I left lame as a reminder that I am forever changed? I can never go back to life as it was. Life will never be the same again.

But the light is calling me, beckoning me toward the memories of the treasures stored away in my heart. There they are – symbols of the life that we shared. Here is the doll, the porcelain doll so lovingly and secretly made as a gift to surprise and please me. Let me touch it. Let me hold it. Let me look at it. Let me have the feel of it next to my cheek. It is beautiful, yet cold and hard, not soft and supple like her flesh. I can never again know that sense of infant-like skin under my fingertips. So I question…did I touch her enough? Did I love her enough? Did I get a fill of the softness of her body, enough to last my lifetime? Her physical presence is removed from me forever. I can never, never again hold her, hug her, and stroke her hair to say I love her. "Parents feel cheated and robbed. They experience an aching sense of incompletion."[73]

I remember my mentor, Marjory, saying, "It was not there, in her room. There was not the presence of the pain of death, only the miraculous glory of God." Death was defeated, for her life is eternal.

I released my quest for answers to unanswerable questions.

Why, oh Lord, why me? Why my daughter? Was I not good enough to be her mother? How could you do this to me? You promised me! You promised me from your Word. You promised me that it was not a sickness unto death, that it would be for your glory. How can that be? How is it possible? She is no longer here. I thought You were going to heal her. Let her walk on this earth to tell of your might and power and healing mercies. That is what I believed. That is what I thought I understood.

What happened? Was I not obedient enough? Was I not kind enough? Did I not love enough? What did I miss? What did I not do that you wanted me to do? I do not understand. All my life, I have been what society considers a good girl. Values from our parents that tell us to be good, do what is right, and trust the Creator are difficult to reconcile when you believe God controls everything and then your child dies. I have followed the rules as best I could. But when I failed, as I often did, I asked you to forgive and to help me along. So, what is it? "Bereaved parents will need guidance in answering those questions that can be answered...and accepting the fact that some cannot be answered or understood."[74]

I left our home. I went into a new environment with her. It was just the two of us, living in a strange land, in a strange house with people we had never met. I left my husband and son to fend for themselves as they worked daily and lived in our home. Why, why was I, were we, separated? Why did I have so much responsibility? It just doesn't seem right. There they are, the men of the family, living and being and moving forward with their lives. **I released my sense of dependency.**

Here we are the women, the ones whose frame is weaker, and the ones who are to be protected and lovingly cared for. Why are we separated to walk this path alone? Is my resentment showing? Is my anger very clear? Living in such a small, small space, when that big house is there. Melanie is calling me. She is calling to me to come and lay down with her, to cuddle up with her. She needs the comfort, the sense of security. But I cannot give it; I cannot go to her just now. I need space, time to think and try to figure out what to do next. Sitting in the darkness, I try to write my thoughts and feelings to protect her from them. I did not want her to sense my pent-up anger, my questions, and my resentment. She had enough burdens to bear – too much, she was only 13 when we were away from home in radiation therapy.

146

I released my resentment over the separation of our family.

Her face was always smiling, pleasant and joyful, unnaturally so even in the face of pain. She thinks of others. Nightly, she prays for the children and parents in the other rooms here. Her spirit is so willing, but her body is so weak from the treatment that is supposed to make her well. She smiles, saying, "Thank you, God, for this treatment. It will make me even better than before. I will be better than before I got this brain tumor. You will take care of me. I know you will." Daily we went into the hospital for radiation treatment, Melanie leaning on my arm in her weakness. Yet she smiled and greeted people as we walked down the hall.

You can see it in their faces, see the questioning look and hear it in their voices as they look at her weakness and say, "Melanie, you seem happy today." And Melanie says, "I am happy. I have the joy of Jesus in my heart. It is his joy that makes me smile." We wait our turn, in the room designed for waiting, with others who have also come for treatment. She looks around the room, choosing to speak with the individuals slumped sadly in their chairs, asking about their day.

Then she is called inside to the huge radiation machine. She yields her small head to be bolted down to the table, to immobilize it for the pinpoint radiation rays to reach their target. It is so exacting that it required expert mathematicians using prescribed formulas to thread the needle to reach the target. One slight movement, even a nanosecond off target would blind her. Her daddy understood; in his earlier years trained as a military sniper, he knew the value of being precisely on target. **I released the images.**

So we listen and we wonder, what does it all mean – the technical words, parts of the anatomy long forgotten after college biology. How were we to understand? We hear, we leave, we wonder. Our son, he understands all too well. Aspiring to be a doctor, already he speaks the medical language. He interprets for us. He helps us understand the criticality of the timing, and the exactness of the procedures. How he ever managed to focus on his studies at Johns Hopkins University in those years I'll never know, except by the grace of God. With his sister's death at the beginning of his fourth year, against all odds, he was able to carry on, to move forward with the life he was called to prepare for. **I released my need to know.**

148

Our son lost more than his sister. We were intentional about maintaining contact, but yet for a time he lost his parents also to their own grief. Society usually gives less attention to siblings than to grieving parents. A surviving child may feel abandoned, by the dead sibling, by the parents and by society. In a sense, we all lost connectedness with each other as individually we sought a reason to get up every day.

My husband had his work, my son had his studies, but I had nothing, or so it seemed, except a sense of emptiness and incompleteness. Why should I struggle to survive the grief that is so painful? Though I will not verbally admit it, my body shows the signs: weight gain, slumped shoulders, folded arms, and that far away, disconnected, confused, questioning look in my eyes. Putting up a good front on the outside, but crying on the inside, raw and bleeding like chopped meat, each wound seared deeply into my being. **I released my regrets over my limited emotional availability to my son and to my husband.**

Resigning myself to fight my own battles while at the same time wondering why I should struggle to survive, I return to my corner of the world, searching, longing, fighting for what I thought I needed. So many memories, so many experiences, private and public locked away to ponder in my heart. It seemed like each was locked in its own tiny treasure chest, some perhaps never to be opened again. With no regard for placement of the keys, I fought the invisible fight, the foe of my inner self, my own dark side that wanted to say, it's not worth it, day after day living with this pain, the pain of separation, the pain of grief that the bereaved are sentenced to endure. It is a lifetime sentence with no hope of being commuted. Harriet Schiff (1977) stated in her book, *The Bereaved Parent,* "To bury a child is to see a part of yourself, your eye color, your dimple, your sense of humor, being placed in the ground. It is life's harshest empathetic experience and must therefore be the hardest one with which to deal."[75] Doubting all I believed, isolating myself, moving numbly in a shattered fragmented world that seemed somewhat familiar, I pressed on with an inner strength that Melanie attested to when she penned a note, "Mama, you have inner strength." Signed, "I love you, Melanie." Is it possible that my daughter, so young in years, but with wisdom beyond her own understanding, saw things in me that I was unaware of myself?

She lived, she loved, she laughed as one from earth, but I wonder if she knew of the impact and influence of her life for years to come. So full of chatter, her brother sometimes referred to her as an "airhead," but when there was a need, he was immediately by her side to protect and care for her.

Her space and place are irreplaceable, they will always be. I can choose to enlarge the capacity of my heart and life to include others and allow the cultivation of new relationships and the rekindling of old ones. But another will never occupy her place, the place of Melanie. **I released the constraints on my heart.**

Your Turn

What intentional action are you prompted to take to release?

What have you been holding on to that you need to release? (thoughts, feelings, bitterness, resentments)

Forgiving is healing.

Will you choose to release it now?

Write, draw, or doodle your thoughts here.
Get up and move – walk, stretch, dance.

THE INTENTIONAL ACTION
OF
CONCLUSION

Now that my daughter has a new dwelling place, I had to make choices. My options were to retreat into the exile of grief, the compelling and easier alternative, or to make the painful, difficult decision to take all she left us and weave it into a new pattern beyond the limits of my imagination. The result has been 23 years of blending, folding, weaving, reweaving, reshaping, redirecting, and reconstructing in such a way that the end product is a composite, but still the mixture is so uniquely mine, I know it cannot be exactly duplicated. The blending, reshaping, reconstructing process will continue as I seek to complete my life story.

When another dies, loving in absence is not so very different from loving in presence. Give and take need not end. We can still give them attention, interest, admiration, understanding, respect, acceptance, forgiveness, loyalty, affection, praise, and gratitude. We can sense that they reciprocate in the living energy of our memory of them. We can receive and still benefit from, for example, material assistance, advice and counsel, instruction, intellectual stimulation, perspective, direction, honesty and candor, moral and spiritual guidance and support, modeling how to be and act, encouragement, expressions of confidence, enthusiasm, a sense of belonging, and inspiration. Some believe our loved ones literally watch over or walk with us. Most of us sense that they are with us in spirit and remain our life's companions in our hearts.

As we relearn the world in which we live, rather than dispose of all that the one we loved meant to us, we embrace the legacies left by them, working toward the creation of a relationship of lasting love, thereby retaining our connection. Choices in maintaining the legacy may include furthering our loved one's interests. When we champion the interests of our loved one, it seems as if they support and/or encourage us.

At Melanie's request we toured the Alamo while in San Antonio, Texas. Construction, steady traffic and uneven sidewalks made pushing her wheelchair a struggle. Attuned to her voice, I could hear sounds, but not distinguish words coming from her. Upon leaning around her I discovered her hands clapping and her voice chanting, "You can do it, Mama. You can do it, Mama. Come on, you can do it, Mama. Yea for Mama." Still today, when I struggle to accomplish a task I discover myself smiling as sometimes I hear the sound of her voice cheering encouragement. Reciprocity changes, it comes in different forms, nevertheless it happens. "Remembering is not a retreat to the past. Rather, memory brings aspects of the past into present awareness."[76]

Melanie left a legacy of love. Her nonjudgmental acceptance, welcoming warmth, concern and compassionate love for others continue to live. Occasionally, I hear stories at church that Melanie was the first to greet someone on their initial visit. The sunshine of her smile brought comfort in a time of uncertainty. Memories that others have may expand or complement the parental memories of the deceased. Remembering is a way of remaining connected to their lives or reconnecting with the reality of those who have died.

Just as Joy, his wife, motivated the author C.S. Lewis to embrace suffering while looking toward future possibilities, Melanie left such strong legacies of serving, loving, caring and compassionate reaching out to help others that she sparked our desire for moving forward into new territory even as we remember life with her. Her life and legacies encourage me to take a risk and try new things, to reach beyond, by perceiving myself entering adventures that, heretofore, I thought were closed to me.

Trying new things requires action. Action requires us to move beyond our comfort zone. It requires intention. Action is the diametric opposite of helplessness. It is a choice. I advocate being intentional about making choices that require action. People may object by saying, "But I am not the same person as you. I do not have resources. That is not me." It was not me either, but I did it, transforming my narrative in the process.

Van's role was interesting throughout this process. The role of the husband and father in this action paradigm is vital. The husband and father must face or refocus his own existence. He and our son continue to nurture a special connection. Our daughter's illness derailed his quick climb to significant wealth. He had to learn quickly how to adapt to change. And yet, I am the only one who knows the magnitude of his support in allowing the wife he married to grow into the woman he could not have foreseen.

Some may say my husband's role was diminished when I moved into forefront of Melanie's rebirthing. However, similar to a Lamaze coach who assists the partner with the pain of childbirth, Van, my coach in this process, supported me emotionally and financially, encouraging me to develop my creative potential through all the avenues that opened up. If he had opposed, contested or exhibited a negative attitude, I would have lost all freedom to move forward, accepting limitations and fighting harder to protect any compatibility in marriage. We remembered the simple promise engraved in our wedding rings: "Each for the Other."

It is apparent to me that this is God's plan and purpose for our lives. It is not of our doing, but that of a higher power. We feel we have no choice except to follow wherever He leads, for whatever reason. I know that He will lead both of us together, not one of us alone, because we made a vow that by the grace of God the oneness of our marriage would survive the tragedy of our daughter's death.

The question has been posed, "Why is Delores making a career out of this?" The question could be phrased differently, "Why is the Creator so insistent on keeping Melanie alive?" "Why did Judas say what Mary did was wasteful" (John 12: 4-6)? Why did Jesus answer, "She did it for me. It will be talked about for years to come" (Mark 14:9)?

Life was not destroyed, but my narrative was completely transformed. As my own interior and exterior landscapes changed, my focus shifted to Melanie's life rather than her death. In this symbolic growth experience there was a shift in my own self-perception from defenselessness, insecurity and ineptitude to self-reliance, self-assurance and competence. Profound appreciation of life and beauty and relationships deepened. Questioning and searching for answers deepened my spiritual growth and trust.

The intentional action of reconstruction, the intentional action of relearning my world, the intentional action of reestablishing relationships, the intentional action of rebirthing a place for my daughter, and the intentional action of reinventing myself contributed to re-creation and discovery of a new equilibrium. Taking intentional action is a daily decision.

There may be a defining moment that initiated the decision, but the choice to follow through is daily. I have learned it is not a matter of thinking less of myself, but thinking of myself less – taking the main focus off my needs and directing toward the needs of others. "Rejoice with them that do rejoice, and weep with them that weep" (Romans 12:14), forgetting myself long enough to lend a helping hand to another.

Upward movement in the School of Suffering brought me and may bring others to a different place in bereavement. Even as we continue to miss the loved one, we learn to give them a difference place in our lives. A widow said, "The bonds of love can never be broken." Death does not sever the love connection, but the connection may change and transition allowing room to love others. We may create new life patterns by folding the

interests and gifts of our loved one with ours.
Nothing remains the same; connections with the
loved one may be lasting, but changed. As we mesh
our life changes with "modified connections with
our family, friends, the larger community, and God.
... We find and make ourselves whole again as
individuals, families, and communities. We blend
the found and the new into unprecedented life
patterns and histories."[77]

I created new ways to complete and re-
create my life story. By opening myself to
vulnerability, it is my deepest desire that others may
be helped to also complete their life stories and
create a new equilibrium for themselves.

Your Turn

What intentional action are you prompted to take to reconstruct your life?

Review them here.

We would like to hear from you!
Send your remarks to drdee@artsasmedicine.com.

EPILOGUE

SERENDIPITY
OF
REVERBRATIONS

Reflectively disclosing and recording my narrative, re-creating my story, and releasing it feels like opening up my heart, exposing it to the world and saying, "Here I am with all my flaws, my hurts, my broken dreams and my shattered world. I invited you in to roam through the fragmented pieces. As you meandered around the shard points and the treacherous curves and the high cliffs, you may have a sense of how I tried to sort through the rubble, salvaging what I could, introducing new parts and pieces as I was able, trying to fit pieces back together in some way to preserve a life. Finally I realized it was not possible to make the pieces fit back together as they were. Eventually I decided that rather than sweeping the fragments into a pile to throw away as trash, I would use an

163

alternate approach. I began a quest to create, using the parts and pieces that remained and introducing new elements. The old and the new pieced together in a pleasing way, forming a kind of 'life mosaic.' Many sharp edges have been smoothed, the cliffs seem to have developed protective fences, and the treacherous curves seem to be banked for safety at controlled speed."

Releasing this manuscript feels like opening myself to naked exposure to the cold north wind. In exposing my vulnerability and honest thoughts and feelings, my greatest hope is that another mother and, indeed, other bereaved people will find the courage to sort through their brokenness and salvage what is usable, then find the courage to risk introducing new elements into life. I also hope that in the process of searching for some meaning in a devastating loss, others will see that jagged pieces can fit together in a new way, as a new creation, into a different, yet beautiful and fully functional life.

It was not until the spring of 1998, when my son said to me, "Mom, I really would like to keep you around as long as I can," that something clicked in my inner being causing me to say, "Yes, I think I'd like to stay." Reflectively, I recognized this as a pivotal moment that sparked my passion to educate the non-bereaved about grief, and to facilitate the process of mourning for the bereaved.

What I have learned I have learned by struggling through a darkness that appeared to be impermeable. The sheer stamina this required is immeasurable. If I had adequate help available, the kind of help I hope to offer to others, perhaps I could have given some things up, i.e. wearing her clothing, opening her birthday gifts. My daughter came out of my physical body, but for me to accomplish the intentional actions for reconstructing meaning after loss, I went into her physical realm. I wonder if this response is totally female.

My purpose in all of this is to be a light at the end of the tunnel for others. I now know that facilitating the grief process requires time, enthusiasm and competence for the long haul. I needed help with learning to live without my daughter. I needed someone who would come alongside of me to help me learn how to act and how to be in a world that was unique to me. I wonder, is maternal bereavement over the loss of a child unlike anything else on earth? I know that parental grief is multifaceted, disrupting every dimension of life.

165

I now know that the grief process is as unique as every individual. I believe every bereaved individual is entitled to have his or her story heard. It is through the telling of the loss experience that others might see through the eyes of grief and feel what it is like for the bereaved, if only for a moment.

At the place where I am now in my transformation, the intensity of emotional pain has lessened; it is no longer frightening and less frequently overwhelming. Over time my grief has changed size and shape and intensity and forms of expression, but it is ever present, attached to me like a shadow. I do not try to explain it away. I do not try to segment it from my life. I have integrated it into every thought and action until it has been woven into the fiber of my being. I no longer deny or run from grief over the death of my daughter. I accept that it will forever be a part of me, and part of me will grieve forever. And that is okay. It has transformed me into who I am and fuels my passion to help others. I have learned to trust, wait, and see life and death from a higher perspective. The waiting times, the solitary times and the sacrifice times have been my growing and learning times.

I have discovered a new equilibrium balanced with giving and receiving.

My grief has softened and I have done a significant amount of grief work; however I still need to publicly acknowledge the life of my daughter. Scholarships and the placement of flowers in church to mark her birthday are samples of continuing public acknowledgment. In the place that I now find myself I no longer attempt to explain the reason behind this need; I just accept that it exists and I act on it.

My sense of being constantly overwhelmed and my tendency toward being overly sensitive and overly reacting to everything have mellowed to a state that now allows relaxation without reprisal. The words Sensei wrote on the first board I broke in karate echo in my thoughts, "Good things can come from a break."

My gift and contribution to the world of grief is to say: "I did it," with Divine intervention, the support of family, friends and my faith community, with medical consultation when necessary, with talk therapy, play therapy, expressive arts therapy, with nutritional therapy and physical exercise therapy, spiritual therapy and, in our own way, marriage therapy, over time. I am a living model that devastating loss can be chiseled, fired and polished until the raw product becomes a multifaceted brilliant jewel or functional vessel. It is possible, with perseverance, determination, and endurance to do more than just survive, but rather to be fully alive and to thrive. I believe life that is celebrated becomes a tribute to the one you love and a gift to the world.

My reason for exposing my vulnerability is in obedience to my calling and in an effort to help others. My authenticity and behavior in speaking with empathy, listening with understanding, accepting with forgiveness and watching with gratitude reflect a transformation in my life and relationships. Grief expression is not "one size fits all." As I strive to balance giving and receiving, it is my privilege as an educator and bereavement facilitator to help others discover methods and strategies for narrative reconstruction and grief expression.

Dr. Dee's Dream

My dream is to have a retreat place where it is safe to pour out the pain of grief.

A haven where the bereaved can open their heart to the real pain they feel.

This is a place where the pain of grief can be constructively expressed through narrative, visual and tactile arts, drama, writing, music and/or movement.

It is a place where Jesus, The Divine Healer can comfort the bereaved through the ministry of believers, counselors or therapists.

At any point along the grief journey toward reconciliation, transformation is possible.

The bereaved will experience forward movement reaching beyond loss and grief toward a new equilibrium.

"Blessed are they that mourn: for they shall be comforted."   *Matthew 5:4 KJV*

The Gulledge Intentional Grief Model

The Intentional Action of **Reconstructing Life.**

The Intentional Action of **Relearning the World.**

The Intentional Action of **Reestablishing Relationships.**

The Intentional Action of **Rebirthing a Place** *for the loved one.*

The Intentional Action of **Reinventing Self.**

Gulledge Expressive Arts Grief Release Plan Arts As Medicine

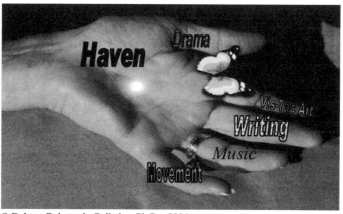

© Delores Dalrymple Gulledge, Ph.D.   2004

"The arts contributed to the transformation of my narrative. They gave form to feelings too deep to articulate and preserved memories too precious to forget."

Dr. Delores D. Gulledge 2005

171

Bibliography

Arvay, M.J. "Shattered beliefs: Reconstituting the self of the trauma counselor." In *Meaning reconstruction & the experience of loss*, edited by R.A. Neimeyer, 213-230. Washington, D.C.: American Psychological Association, 2001.

Attig, T. "Relearning the world: Making and finding meanings." In *Meaning reconstruction & the experience of loss*, edited by R.A. Neimeyer, 157-172. Washington, D.C.: American Psychological Association, 2001.

Attig, T. *The heart of grief: Death and the search for lasting love*. New York: Oxford University Press, 2000.

Bloomfield, J. *Other ways of knowing: Recharting our future with ageless wisdom*. Rochester, N.Y.: Inner Traditions, 1997.

Bright, R. *Grief and Powerlessness: Helping people regain control of their lives*. London: Jessica Kingsley Publishers, 1996.

Calhoun, L.G. and Tedeschi, R.G. "Posttraumatic growth: The positive lessons of loss." In *Meaning reconstruction & the experience of loss,* edited by R.A. Neimeyer, 157-172. Washington, D.C.: American Psychological Association, 2001.

Carney, E.M. "Don't waste your life." Columbia, S.C.: Unpublished manuscript, 2004. www.riverlandhills.org

Davies, B., Gudmundsdottir, M., Worden, B., Orloff, S., Sumner, L., & Brenner, P. "Living in the dragon's shadow: A father's experiences of a child's life-limiting illness." *Death Studies 28(2)* (2004): 111-135.

Davis, C. G. "The tormented and the transformed: Understanding responses to loss and trauma." In *Meaning reconstruction & the experience of loss,* edited by R.A. Neimeyer, 137-155. Washington, D.C.: American Psychological Association, 2001.

Ellenburg, J.S.W. "Melanie's miracle celebration." In *G.F.A. friends.* Columbia, S.C.: Unpublished manuscript, 1990.

Frantz, T.T., Farrell, M.M., & Trolley, B.C. *Positive outcomes of losing a loved one.* Washington, D.C.: American Psychological Association, 2002.

Keleman, S. *Embodying experience: Forming a personal life.* Berkeley, Calif.: Center Press, 1987.

King, L.A. "Gain without pain? Expressive writing and self-regulation." In *The writing cure: How expressive writing promotes health and emotional well-being,* edited by S.J. Lepore & J.M. Smyth, 119-134. Washington: American Psychological Association, 2002.

Klass, D. "The inner representation of the dead child in the psychic and social narratives of bereaved parents." In *Meaning reconstruction & the experience of loss*, edited by R.A. Neimeyer, 113-134. Washington, D.C.: American Psychological Association, 2001.

Larson, D.G. & Scro, R. *The caring helper*. (VHS) Santa Clara: 1991.

Mathes, C.M. *The experience of mothers who have suffered the death of a child: A heuristic study*. Unpublished dissertation, Union Institute & University, 1999.

McGarth, P. "Religiosity and the challenge of terminal illness." *Death Studies 27(10)* (2003): 881-99.

McNiff, S. *Art-based research*. Philadelphia, Penn.: Jessica Kingsley Publishers, 1998.

Milo, E.M. "The death of a child with a developmental disability." In *Meaning reconstruction & the experience of loss*, edited by R.A. Neimeyer, 113-134. Washington, D.C.: American Psychological Association, 2001.

Nadeau, J.W. "Family construction of meaning." In *Meaning reconstruction & the experience of loss*, edited by R.A. Neimeyer, 95-111. Washington, D.C.: American Psychological Association, 2001.

Neimeyer, R.A. *Meaning reconstruction & the experience of loss*. Washington, D.C.: American Psychological Association, 2001.

Rando, T.A., ed. *Parental loss of a child*. Champaign, Ill: Research Press Company, 1986.

Roseman, J.L. *The way of the woman writer* (2nd ed.). Binghamton: Hawthorne Press, Inc., 2003.

Sewell, K.W., & Williams, A.M. "Construing stress: A constructivist therapeutic approach to posttraumatic stress reactions." In *Meaning reconstruction & the experience of loss*, edited by R.A. Neimeyer, 293-310. Washington, D.C.: American Psychological Association, 2001.

Stroebe, M. & Schut, H. "Meaning making in the dual process model of coping with bereavement." In *Meaning reconstruction & the experience of loss*, edited by R.A. Neimeyer, 55-73. Washington, D.C.: American Psychological Association, 2001.

Worden, J.W. *Grief counseling and grief therapy: A handbook for the mental health practitioner* (3rd ed.). New York: Springer, 2002.

ENDNOTES

Chapter 1 – The Action of Survival

[1] E.M. Milo, "The death of a child with a developmental disability," in *Meaning reconstruction & the experience of loss*, ed. R.A. Neimeyer (Washington, D.C.: American Psychological Association, 2001), 113-134.

Chapter 2 – The Intentional Action of Reconstructing Life

[2] E.M. Carney, "Don't waste your life" (Columbia, S.C.: Unpublished manuscript, 2004).

[3] T.A. Rando, ed., *Parental loss of a child* (Champaign, Ill.: Research Press Company, 1986), 476.

[4] B. Davies et. al., "Living in the dragon's shadow: A father's experiences of a child's life-limiting illness," *Death Studies 28*(2) (2004): 115.

[5] C. G. Davis, "The tormented and the transformed: Understanding responses to loss and trauma," in *Meaning reconstruction & the experience of loss*, ed. R.A. Neimeyer (Washington, D.C.: American Psychological Association, 2001), 140.

[6] Rando, 305.

[7] D. Klass, "The inner representation of the dead child in the psychic and social narratives of bereaved parents," in *Meaning reconstruction & the experience of loss*, ed. R.A. Neimeyer (Washington, D.C.: American Psychological Association, 2001), 82.

[8] T. Attig, "Relearning the World: Making and Finding Meanings," in *Meaning reconstruction & the experience of loss*, ed. R.A. Neimeyer (Washington, D.C.: American Psychological Association, 2001), 41.

[9] M.J. Arvay, "Shattered beliefs: Reconstituting the self of the trauma counselor," in *Meaning reconstruction & the experience of loss*, ed. R.A. Neimeyer (Washington, D.C.: American Psychological Association, 2001), 223.

[10] K.W. Sewell and A.M. Williams, "Construing stress: A constructivist therapeutic approach to posttraumatic stress reactions," in *Meaning reconstruction & the experience of loss*, ed. R.A. Neimeyer (Washington, D.C.: American Psychological Association, 2001), 297.

Chapter 3 – The Intentional Action of Relearning My World

[11] Attig, 42.
[12] Ibid., 43.
[13] Ibid., 41.
[14] J.W. Worden, *Grief counseling and grief therapy: A handbook for the mental health practitioner (3rd edition)* (New York: Springer, 2002), 154.
[15] Attig, 43.
[16] Ibid., 41-2.
[17] T. Attig, *The heart of grief: Death and the search for lasting love* (New York: Oxford University Press, 2000), 200.
[18] Ibid, 200.
[19] Attig, 40.

Chapter 4 – The Intentional Action of Re-Establishing Relationships

[20] Ibid., 40.
[21] R.A. Neimeyer, *Meaning reconstruction & the experience of loss* (Washington, D.C.: American Psychological Association, 2001), 267.
[22] T.A. Rando, ed., *Parental loss of a child* (Champaign, Ill.: Research Press Company, 1986), 38.

[23] Rando, 39.
[24] Attig, 44.
[25] Rando, 475.
[26] Neimeyer, 266.
[27] Rando, 476.
[28] Neimeyer, 266.

[29] D. Klass, "The inner representation of the dead child in the psychic and social narratives of bereaved parents," in *Meaning reconstruction & the experience of loss*, ed. R.A. Neimeyer (Washington, D.C.: American Psychological Association, 2001), 85.

[30] Attig, 44.

[31] T.T. Frantz, et. al., *Positive outcomes of losing a loved one* (Washington, D.C.: American Psychological Association, 2002), 193.

[32] L.G. Calhoun and R.G. Tedeschi, "Posttraumatic growth: The positive lessons of loss," in *Meaning reconstruction & the experience of loss*, ed. R.A. Neimeyer (Washington, D.C.: American Psychological Association, 2001), 160.

[33] Calhoun & Tedeschi,160.

[34] E.M. Milo, "The death of a child with a developmental disability," in *Meaning reconstruction & the experience of loss*, ed. R.A. Neimeyer (Washington, D.C.: American Psychological Association, 2001), 125.

[35] Attig, 52.

[36] Rando, 25.

[37] J.W. Worden, *Grief counseling and grief therapy: A handbook for the mental health practitioner* (3rd ed.) (New York: Springer, 2002), 157.

[38] Frantz, 193-4.

[39] P. McGarth, "Religiosity and the challenge of terminal illness," *Death Studies 27*(10) (2003): 894.

[40] Rando, 476.

[41] See inset, "Ethereal Dancer," and photograph.

Chapter 5 – The Intentional Action of Rebirthing a Place for Melanie

[42] J. W. Nadeau, "Family construction of meaning," in *Meaning reconstruction & the experience of loss*, ed. R.A. Neimeyer (Washington, D.C.: American Psychological Association, 2001), 103.

[43] Attig, 37, 46.

[44] Klass, 77.

[45] Attig, 49.

Chapter 6 – The Intentional Action of Reinventing Myself

[46] C.M. Mathes, *The experience of mothers who have suffered the death of a child: A heuristic study* (Dissertation, Union Institute & University, 1999), 26.

[47] Attig, 40.

[48] Davis, 149.

[49] Attig, 34.

[50] D.G. Larson & R. Scro, *The caring helper* (VHS) (Santa Clara: 1991).

[51] Davis, 138.

[52] Calhoun & Tedeschi, 157.

[53] L.A. King, "Gain without pain? Expressive writing and self-regulation." In *The writing cure: How expressive writing promotes health and emotional well-being*, S.J. Lepore & J.M. Smyth (eds.) (Washington: American Psychological Association, 2002), 122.

[54] J.L. Roseman, *The way of the woman writer* (2nd ed.). (Binghamton: Hawthorne Press, Inc., 2003), 1.

[55] Calhoun & Tedeschi, 158.

[56] Milo, 120.

[57] Rando, 305.

[58] Frantz, et. al., 194.

[59] M. Stroebe & H. Schut, "Meaning making in the dual process model of coping with bereavement," in *Meaning reconstruction & the experience of loss*, ed. R.A. Neimeyer (Washington, D.C.: American Psychological Association, 2001), 67.

[60] J.S.W. Ellenburg, "Melanie's miracle celebration," in *G.F.A. Friends* (Columbia, S.C.: Unpublished manuscript, 1990).

[61] Worden, 19.

[62] Klass, 93.

[63] Frantz, et. al, 192.

[64] Klass, 90.

[65] Ibid., 91.

[66] R. Bright, *Grief and Powerlessness: Helping people regain control of their lives* (London: Jessica Kingsley Publishers, 1996), 5.

Chapter 7 – The Intentional Action of Re-creating the Story through "Griefsong"

[67] J. Bloomfield, *Other ways of knowing: Recharting our future with ageless wisdom* (Rochester, N.Y.: Inner Traditions, 1997), 97.
[68] S. McNiff, *Art-based research* (Philadelphia, Penn.: Jessica Kingsley Publishers, 1998), 85.
[69] S. Keleman, *Embodying experience: Forming a personal life* (Berkeley, Calif.: Center Press, 1987), 1.
[70] McNiff, 2.
[71] Keleman, 53.

Chapter 8 – The Intentional Action of Releasing the Story through "Griefsong"

[72] Rando, 299.

Chapter 9 – The Intentional Action of Expressing Deep Personal Feelings through "Griefsong"

[73] Rando, 11.
[74] Rando, 399.
[75] Rando, 313.

Chapter 10 – Conclusion

[76] Attig, 48.
[77] Attig, 52.

About the Author

Over time, it became very clear that academic credentials were to be added to personal experience to fulfill and validate a mother's promise to her daughter. Without question, God was in control and guided every element of the process. Dee's mission and life purpose is to teach and to comfort others as she has been taught and comforted. To be the ears that listen, the eyes that see, the touch that comforts, the fragrance that sweetens, the taste of salt that renews a thirst for life. To be the expression of a loving God to a hurting world, pointing the way to the Source of comfort and strength and life.

Dr. Delores Dalrymple Gulledge, Thanatologist; Bereavement Management Specialist, is an educator and research practitioner who uses the expressive arts as a method of intervention for intense emotions often associated with loss and grief. Her innovative approach to reconciliation of grief through using the Arts As Medicine has proven to be beneficial to bereaved individuals. She is a popular conference presenter, seminar speaker, and workshop and retreat leader.

Dee Gulledge is associated with the Richland County Coroner–Medical Examiner's Office in South Carolina as a Deputy Coroner and C.A.R.E. Team Coordinator. She is a Community Crisis Response trainer with the National Organization of Victim Assistance and with South Carolina Baptist Disaster Relief.

Also, she is on the Brain Tumor Advisory Board of Duke University Medical Center; Leadership Council of the University of South Carolina Cancer Research Center; Board of Visitors and adjunct faculty at Columbia College in Columbia, SC.

Dr. Gulledge is co-founder of The Other Side Ministries, Inc.; and founder of ICARE Resources, Inc. Her grief practice, Arts As Medicine, LLC is located at 1929 Gadsden St., Columbia, SC 29201.

Additionally, she is a member of: Association for Death Education and Counseling; National Organization for Victim Assistance; International Expressive Arts Therapy Association; South Carolina Coroners Association; International Association of Coroners & Medical Examiners.

Delores and Van Gulledge, intimately acquainted with grief and loss, struggled to put their world back together after the death of their teenage daughter, Melanie.

Personal loss, family tragedy, relationally estranged, emotionally depleted, financially drained, shaken to their foundation, but not destroyed, the "God of all Comfort" sustained them through the valley of the shadow of darkness.

With Intentional Action they regained stability and discovered a new equilibrium for their lives. Repairing relationships, attending to the soul's deep wounds, reorganizing daily activities, and reaching out to give solace to others from the experience of their pain provided a healing balm that gave strength to their weary hearts.

As God has held the family with a love that will not let go, they highly regard the memory and experiences with their beautiful beloved daughter through scholarships and memorials.

Their son pursued his calling into medicine earning degrees from The Johns Hopkins University, The Medical University of South Carolina, Duke University, and the University of North Carolina at Chapel Hill. Currently, he is a forensic pathologist and medical examiner. His wife studied at The Johns Hopkins University, Thomas Jefferson University and the University of North Carolina at Chapel Hill. She is a research scientist.

Van and Dee have been blessed with 48 years of marriage; a son, a daughter-in-law and their daughter, Melanie. For more than 40 years they have been active members of Riverland Hills Baptist Church, near Columbia, South Carolina.

To reserve speaking engagements, workshops, seminars, retreats, etc., contact:

Dr. Gulledge
Arts as Medicine, llc
Telephone: (803) 730-2220
E-mail: drdee@artsasmedicine.com